Secrets
Transforming Your Life and Marriage

Kerry Clarensau

GPH
Gospel Publishing House
Springfield, Missouri

02-0505

This book contains contact information for private and public organizations other than Gospel Publishing House. The contact information is not intended as endorsement of any product, service, or expressed view, or for Web site performance provided by these third party entities. Gospel Publishing House is not responsible for the advice, content, or performance of linked sites or phone numbers; access at your own risk.

2nd Printing 2010

ISBN 978-0-88243-811-5

Printed in United States of America

Lindsey's Story

As the product of abuse, addiction, and a broken home, I was overwhelmed and confused in my new marriage. I knew all the wifely ideals—I grew up in church and had a degree in Christian Counseling. But I didn't know how to reach these ideals. I battled dissatisfaction, emotional ups and downs, and had difficulty connecting with my husband. I wished someone could tell me if my struggles were normal and how to handle them. I remember pouring out these frustrations in my journal one evening: *What's wrong with me? Why do I feel this way? Lord, I'm so confused! What is healthy and what is not? Who can I trust to even ask?*

From the first page of *Secrets*, I was amazed at Kerry's honesty and insight. She became the friend I prayed for, and guided me through the key issues every wife faces. But the real power in this book is that it's based on the Bible. As I applied God's truth to my heart, I drew closer to Him and saw Him work in my marriage. The process was not always easy—I had to take personal responsibility, get really honest with myself, and admit where I'm self-focused. I had to unlearn the philosophies from our culture and align myself with God's truth. But God held me each step of the way.

After finishing *Secrets*, I happened to read my old journal. Then it hit me—*I haven't felt those emotions in months! There is so much peace in my heart and in my marriage!* God has brought me so far; I no longer blame my past, my husband, and my circumstances. Instead, I focus on what I can change—me, and I let God do the rest. Now, my husband and I are closer and more honest with each other than we've ever been. I talk to him about issues I used to hide, and I understand and appreciate him more.

Of course, I still encounter struggles, but I have the secrets to navigate through them. I am so thankful for this book—*Secrets* has changed the destiny of my life and marriage!

Lindsey

Gary's Story

For thirty-eight years I tried to change my wife and met only with marital tension. All those years I wanted her to exercise every day with me and for us to eat better together. In those two areas, I was always on her case, critical and judgmental, thinking no one else could change her but me.

Finally one night at dinner I said, "There's something I've been doing that I want to ask your forgiveness for." She looked a bit apprehensive until I explained, "For thirty-eight years, I've been sinning against you and trying to adjust you in several areas. Will you forgive me for the many times I tried to change you and not accept you for exactly who you are?"

I said to her, "My promise to you today is that I'm only going to work on me."

That was a turning point. I began focusing on the areas I needed to change and letting God work in my heart.

Four years later, guess what happened? She started eating right and exercising with me! For years I couldn't get her to do it, but now she's committed.

What made the difference? I got off her case, and she and God worked it all out, while I was oblivious. He did it all, helping her to take responsibility for her health. That's the kind of miracle that comes when you take care of yourself and trust your mate to God. That's the kind of miracle you can expect in your marriage through *Secrets*.

Throughout my years as a relationship counselor, I've learned every marriage will benefit from the wisdom in these pages. As a husband, I know firsthand the impact that you, as a wife, can have on your husband when you work on yourself. You'll discover the essential secrets every wife needs to build a great marriage. From relying on God to be your source, to meeting your husband's greatest need, to growing more deeply in love—*Secrets* has them all.

As you journey through *Secrets*, I pray God will transform your life and marriage as you allow the Holy Spirit to change your heart. Expect a miracle!

Dr. Gary Smalley
Author and relationship expert
Smalley Relationship Center
Branson, Missouri

Kerry's Story

As a pastor's wife, I have the privilege of walking with women in all stages of life and marriage. From offering premarital counseling to having coffee with women who have been married for forty years, I see upclose the challenges wives faces.

So many of our struggles are private, like the desire to find true fulfillment, overcome temptation, or reject our culture's self-focused view of love. And on some level, we all must work to understand and really appreciate our husbands.

Other trials are more visible and life altering. While my husband and I are pastors—not professional counselors—we do what I call "emergency room" counseling. We tend to be the first call when people learn their spouse is unfaithful, is viewing pornography, or decides they don't want to be married any longer.

Bookstores are filled with marriage materials for couples, but there are few resources written solely for wives. I wrote *Secrets* because I care deeply about the women in our church, community, and you! Our culture simply doesn't prepare us to be a successful wife. But God's Word is full of life-giving secrets that can be applied specifically to our role as a wife. I want to come along-side those I love and help them to take a close look at these transforming secrets!

Every secret shared in this study has been discovered on my own journey of seeking God and sharing life with my wonderful husband, Mike. We have experienced countless joys and faced many challenges. Yet together, we have allowed the truth of God's Word to transform our individual lives which has transformed our relationship. I'm so thankful for him and the love we share.

Friend, I am excited for what God is about to do in *your* life. Despite the ways your personality, past experiences, or mistakes may have impacted your marriage, you will discover how you can follow God's design. He will help you to experience fulfillment and joy in the most important position you will fill in life. I pray as you journey through these studies, you will allow God's Word to change your thoughts, attitudes, and actions—and transform your marriage!

Kerry Clarensau
Author of *Secrets*

Contents

Acknowledgements

I am always amazed at how God puts all the pieces together. Last year, He brought an incredible editorial assistant into my life—Lindsey Parsons. Her ability with words and amazing organizational skills blessed me every step of the way! As a newlywed, her fresh perspective and probing questions created unique insights. *Secrets* wouldn't be the same without her.

Darla Knoth, senior editor, spent numerous hours editing this study after she led a small group to pilot the material. Working on *Secrets* with Darla was like spending time with a dear friend. She is a gifted editor and gracious wife! I would like to thank everyone who participated in Darla's small group— Arlene, Karlene, Jennifer, Joy, Lindsey, Patty, and Debbie. They experienced *Secrets* in its roughest form and helped to shape this material.

Frank Gamble and his crew at OneStone Media, along with the talented project team at Gospel Publishing House, believed in this project and used their individual gifts to make *Secrets* the best it could be.

This study wouldn't be complete without the amazing insights from Gary Smalley. Not only is he a relationship expert, but his spiritual maturity and ongoing pursuit of God were inspiring and refreshing. He was a pleasure to work with, and I'm so grateful for the humble transparency he showed.

The women of Maranatha Worship Center in Wichita, Kansas, contributed to this project in immeasurable ways. Whether it was over coffee, in a small group, or in a classroom full of women, they allowed me to "think out loud." Each of them inspires and challenges me in some way. What amazing women! They will see reflections of our journey together in each session.

Every one mentioned in this list has contributed to this Bible study. But even more importantly, they have prayed for you! Together we have prayed that you will allow God's truth to change your life and transform your marriage!

Want to Hear a Secret?

Every woman loves a secret! We want to know the secret ingredients of a friend's best recipe, or the secret to managing a chaotic schedule. We like secrets because they tell us that a friend trusts us with her privileged feelings or information.

What if you could find secrets just for wives—finding true fulfillment, understanding your husband, meeting his greatest need, connecting more intimately, staying in love? You may be thinking, *Wow, if those secrets could only be found.*

They can be found! This book is filled with those secrets. However, they're not secrets because they're hard to find; they're secrets because so many people still haven't heard about them. But you can! God has revealed these secrets to all of us in the Bible—His written revelation of life and how it's to be lived. As the Author of marriage, God knows what will make marriages fulfilling and lasting. He doesn't expect us to make it up as we go or simply to try our best. His plan is for us to study, to know His Word, and then to teach each other (Titus 2:1–5).

That's why the *Secrets* book you are holding is so exciting! It is specially designed for a women-only environment, where you can discuss truths from God's Word and apply them specifically to your role as a wife. You will enjoy using *Secrets* for individual study, one-on-one mentoring, or in a small group.

This book will help you take responsibility for the part you play in your marriage. This is not a manual on how to fix your husband. But by focusing on your own growth and change, you will open the way for God to work in your marriage. If you are:

- a woman planning to marry (or remarry) someday
- a wife enjoying the first years of marriage

- a wife raising school-age children
- a wife experiencing the empty nest
- a wife facing marital struggles
- a wife whose husband has yet to follow Jesus

. . . then this study is for you!

This book contains questions to stimulate discussion and places for you to journal your thoughts. The section, *Just between You and God,* is designed to help you take the truths of each session and apply them specifically to your life and marriage.

Questions for *Just between You and Your Husband* are designed to enhance communication between the two of you. However, since every marriage relationship is different, prayerfully consider if these questions would be beneficial for your relationship. If not, then feel free to skip that section.

As you begin this journey, keep in mind that the effort put into any study will determine how much you get out of it. A perfect example of this is Katie, a young nursing student. God challenged her to take this study as seriously as her nursing classes. She realized that her role as a wife is more important than her role as a nurse. Katie devoted herself to look up all the Scripture references, to journal her responses to all the questions, to memorize Scripture, and to pray for her husband daily. She was amazed and thankful for the transformation that took place in her life and marriage. May Katie's challenge become yours—look forward to transformation!

Session 1.

The SECRET to Finding True Fulfillment
Allowing God to Meet Your Deepest Needs

"Satisfy us in the morning with your unfailing love,
that we may sing for joy and be glad all of our days."
Psalm 90:14

Think about It . . .

Did you ever daydream about the man who would sweep you off your feet? Most of us can admit we've spent time imagining what our husband would be like. We might have even written a list of the characteristics we hoped he would have—taking the best features of the guys we knew and combining them into our ideal man. We probably even had our own ideas about how he would express his undying love to us.

As a single woman, how did you describe your ideal man?

_____

_____

_____

_____

_____

What I've Discovered about Unrealistic Expectations

It's embarrassing to admit, but some of those "daydreamy" ideas followed me right into my marriage. As a young bride, I thought, *My husband will not only make me happy and provide for me, he will understand my deepest thoughts and emotions. We will enjoy at least one romantic evening every week for the rest of our lives. And those few things I don't like about him, I'm sure I'll be able to change!*

With a little more maturity, I began to understand that it was pretty unrealistic for me to think any man could live up to my list of expectations. But even with this understanding, I can easily slip into having other unrealistic ideas like:

- *My husband should know how I need him to respond.*
- *This marriage should be so much easier.*
- *If he really loved me, my husband would . . .*

Simply trying to adjust my expectations didn't bring fulfillment. I found myself thinking, *Okay, it isn't possible for one man to meet all of my needs—but surely having children, a home, education, a career, accomplishments, and experiences will bring fulfillment.* While all of these are blessings to enjoy, they didn't bring the satisfaction I was craving.

Where do people look to find fulfillment?

_____

_____

_____

_____

In order to discover the secret to true fulfillment, we must understand what our real needs are and who can meet them.

What Are Our Deepest Needs?

In *Marriage on the Rock,* Jimmy and Karen Evans detail four basic needs everyone seeks to satisfy throughout life:

- **security** (knowing we are cared for)
- **identity** (knowing who we are)
- **acceptance** (knowing that we belong)
- **purpose** (knowing that we matter)[1]

When we were children, parents or caregivers played an important role in meeting these needs in a very basic way. As we grew into adulthood, those needs began to change and deepen.

Which one of these four needs is most important to you?

_____

Which of these four needs do you struggle with the most?

_____

Although I accepted Jesus as my Savior at a young age, I didn't understand the depth of the relationship He offered me. While I knew the things I should and shouldn't do, I didn't enjoy a close relationship with Him. I was completely unaware that Jesus was able to satisfy my heart and meet my deepest needs.

So when I met and married Mike, most of those unmet needs were transferred to my relationship with him. Poor guy! He probably didn't know what to do with his needy young bride.

How Can God Meet Our Deepest Needs?

God is so faithful! A couple of years after we were married, Mike and I did an in-depth study of the Book of Psalms. As I saw the open, honest way the Psalmist approached God, I began to understand the type of relationship He offers me. It was an amazing discovery—the all-powerful, all-knowing, ever-present, and loving God wants us to run into His presence with every question, fear, and emotion. He wants to be our closest friend and meet our deepest needs.

Now years later as my relationship with God continues to grow, I experience more and more contentment. I've discovered the amazing truth of Philippians 4:19—"And my God will meet all your needs according to his glorious riches in Christ Jesus."

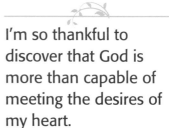

I'm so thankful to discover that God is more than capable of meeting the desires of my heart.

Let's consider how God is the source for meeting our deepest needs.

Security ➤ Knowing that we are cared for

God alone is our security and our safe place. In Psalm 62:5, David expressed it this way:

> Find rest, O my soul, in God alone; my hope comes from him. He alone is my rock and my salvation; he is my fortress, I will not be shaken. My salvation and my honor depend on God; he is my mighty rock, my refuge. Trust in him at all times, O people; pour out your hearts to him, for God is our refuge.

God is all-powerful, all-knowing, and ever-present. Why should we fear? Notice that He wants us to "pour out" our heart to Him. We can take absolutely everything to Him. We are safe and secure in His loving arms.

Identity ⤐ Knowing who we are

We gain a new identity the moment we accept Jesus as our Savior. First John 3:1 tells us:

> How great is the love the Father has lavished on us, that we should be called children of God! And that is what we are!

What an incredible reality: we are the children of God! We should seek to discover all it means to be called His *child*. Our identity is in Him, and not in our abilities, positions, possessions, or relationships.

Acceptance ⤐ Knowing that we belong

We can find no greater acceptance than what the words of Isaiah 43:1 describe:

> But now, this is what the Lord says—he who created you, O Jacob . . . "Fear not, for I have redeemed you; I have summoned you by name; you are mine."

We can be assured that those words are for anyone redeemed by the sacrifice of Jesus. God says to us, "You are mine." He has called us His own. Once we begin to discover the depths of His great love for us, our need for acceptance will be met in the deepest part of our being.

Purpose ⤐ Knowing that we matter

True fulfillment is found as you submissively walk with God and allow His purpose to be fulfilled in your life. We learn this from David, the second king of Israel. (His story can be read in the Old Testament in 1 and 2 Samuel. God chose David to be king because he was a man after God's own heart.) David was so certain that God would reveal His purpose for his life that he wrote these words in Psalm 138:8.

> The LORD will fulfill his purpose for me; your love, O LORD, endures forever—do not abandon the works of your hands.

We were lovingly created by God for a specific purpose. He uniquely designed us to carry out His individual plans for our lives. God doesn't create duplicates, so we shouldn't compare our role to others. We are the only person who can do what we were created to do.

Think about the need you struggle with the most. How can God meet that need?

_____

_____

_____

How Should We Respond to Discontentment?

Anytime I begin to feel discontent, I've learned to search my heart and see if I'm expecting someone or something else to meet my needs. Since Mike is my closest human relationship, I often misplace my expectations onto him. I must continually remind myself that only God can heal my brokenness and meet the deepest needs of my heart.

To help me do that, I ask myself the following questions:

- **Is there unconfessed sin in my life?**
  Unconfessed sin causes us to feel troubled and unsettled. "When I refused to confess my sin, my body wasted away, and I groaned all day long" (Psalm 32:3, NLT). Read Psalm 32 to understand the joy repentance brings.

  > Discontentment can be a spiritual alarm calling us to draw closer to God.

  Answer: _____

  _____

- **Am I seeking to really *know* God, or am I simply seeking what He can *do* for me?**
  In Psalm 27:8, David speaks of seeking God's *face*—wanting to truly know Him. But many times we seek God's *hand*—only wanting what He can do for us. We approach Him like a vending machine, "God, give me this, I'll take a double portion of that." However, when we keep seeking to really know God, we will experience a closeness that will satisfy the deepest places in our heart.

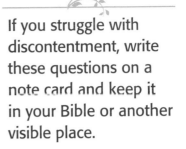

If you struggle with discontentment, write these questions on a note card and keep it in your Bible or another visible place.

  Answer: _____

  _____

- **Am I failing to trust God completely?**
  In Psalms, David shows us that God alone was his Source. When we depend on anything or anyone else, we are disappointed. Read Psalm 33:21,22 to understand the joy of trusting in God.

  Answer: _____

  _____

- **Do I have unresolved emotions?**
  When we experience overwhelming emotions, our first response may be to try to resolve them on our own. But when we pour out all of our emotions to God, we find complete resolve and healing. He gives us the right perspective and new insights. Read Psalm 31:9–24 to see how David expressed his anguish, and then trusted God to take care of him.

  Answer: _____

  _____

- **Am I living unaware of God's presence?**

  When we live continually aware of God's presence, we can enjoy fellowship with Him throughout our day. We find security and peace when we realize that He is present in every situation. We can find rest in the assurance that we are never alone. Read Psalm 139:5–18 to hear David's description of God's presence.

  Answer: _____

  _____

- **Am I grateful or grumbling?**

  Gratefulness and discontentment cannot coexist. A thankful heart is focused on the goodness and blessings of God, rather than what is lacking. Read Psalm 95:1–7 to see the power of thanking and praising God.

  Answer: _____

  _____

How Can We Adjust Our Expectations?

This has been an incredible journey for me. When I accepted that God alone is my Source, I began to seek Him and allowed Him to meet my deepest needs. The fulfillment that I found allowed me to remove unrealistic expectations from my husband. Then he was free to meet the needs he was created to meet, and we grew closer.

The amazing thing about the contentment God brings is that it satisfies even when our realistic expectations go unmet.

> A woman needs a simple but deep belief in her heart that God is the only Source of her life, and He is capable of meeting all of her needs.
>
> Gary Smalley, *Secrets* DVD

How I've Adjusted My Expectations

It is unrealistic and unhealthy to expect that ...	*It is realistic and healthy to expect that ...*
• My husband should meet *all* my relational needs.	• My husband is my most important human relationship. But God has promised never to leave me or forsake me.
• My husband should provide complete financial security.	• My husband and I will work together and trust God to provide for our family.
• My husband should understand my feelings and know what I am thinking.	• My husband and I will grow in our understanding of one another. But God knows and understands all my thoughts.
• My husband should make me happy.	• My husband can provide support and encouragement; true joy is found in a right relationship with God.
• My husband should make me feel good about myself.	• I am fully responsible for my thoughts and feelings, and my husband can support and love me.
• My husband should always respond the way I want him to.	• My husband will respond in a way that is consistent with who he is.
• My husband will never disappoint me.	• My husband will make mistakes and sometimes disappoint me. Only God is perfect.

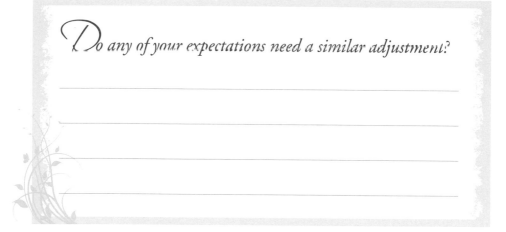

Do any of your expectations need a similar adjustment?

The Secret to Finding True Fulfillment

We've discovered that true fulfillment cannot be found until we experience closeness with God. Sincerely seeking Him will reap wonderful benefits—He will heal our brokenness and meet all our needs.

When we embrace this truth, we will find joy and peace no matter what stage of life we are in. And we will free our husband from God-sized responsibilities. Then, something amazing will happen in our marriage.

> God's unfailing love can satisfy my deepest needs.

- *We will begin to see our husband differently.* Instead of focusing on how our husband fails to live up to our expectations, we will appreciate him for who he is.

- *We will begin to look different to our husband.* Instead of seeing our discontented spirit, he will see the beauty of a quiet spirit as we trust God to meet our deepest needs (1 Peter 3:4).

Verses to Remember

"Find rest, O my soul, in God alone; my hope comes from him. He alone is my rock and my salvation; he is my fortress, I will not be shaken. My salvation and my honor depend on God; he is my mighty rock, my refuge. Trust in him at all times, O people; pour out your hearts to him, for God is our refuge" (Psalm 62:5–8).

Prayer

Heavenly Father, thank You for loving me and offering me a relationship that can satisfy the deepest needs of my heart. Forgive me for expecting someone or something else to bring fulfillment. Help me not to place unrealistic expectations on my husband—frustrating him and leaving me unfulfilled. Help me to find fulfillment in You, and free me to love my husband with Your unconditional love. Amen.

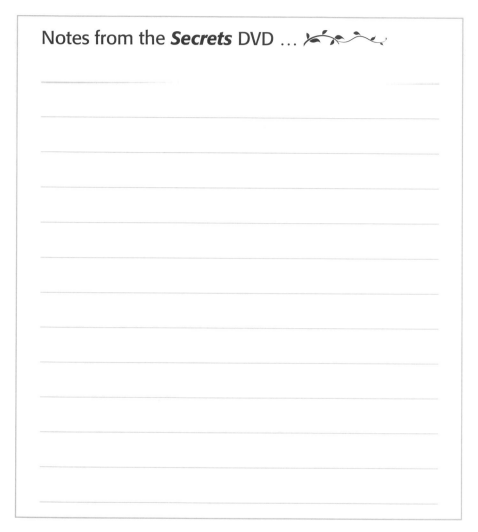

Notes from the *Secrets* DVD ...

Meet Liz ...

She thought her second husband—a marriage and family therapist—would meet her deepest needs and erase the abuse from her first marriage. But she soon realized that her impossible expectations were pushing her husband away from her. On a journey toward finding true fulfillment, God healed Liz's brokenness and transformed her marriage. Hear her story on the *Secrets* DVD.

Just between You and God

- Which part of this session spoke the most to you and why?

- How fulfilling is your relationship with God? If you would like to know more about following Jesus, read Appendix A, "Following Jesus."

- Are you feeling discontent in any area of your life? If so, recognize this might be a spiritual alarm calling you to draw closer to God. Turn back to the section "How Should We Respond to Discontentment?" and take time to answer the questions in the space provided.

- Ask God to show you if you have placed unrealistic expectations on your husband—whether expecting him to meet God-sized needs or expecting him to measure up to your idea of the perfect husband.

- Take time this week to pray using Appendix B, "Prayer Guides," and journal specific prayers and Scriptures for your husband and yourself.

Just between You and Your Husband

- Suggested Discussion Starter: Ask your husband, "Can you describe the last time you felt that I placed unrealistic expectations on you?"

- Suggested Discussion Starter: Ask your husband, "How did my expectations make you want to respond?"

- Turn back to the section "How Can We Adjust Our Expectations?" and read the chart. Together make a list of healthy expectations for one another. (Examples: My wife is my best friend, not my fishing buddy. My husband and I will work on the budget together.)

Husband: _____

_____

_____

_____

_____

_____

Wife: _____

_____

_____

_____

_____

_____

_____

Session 2

The SECRET to Embracing His Differences

Understanding and Appreciating the Differences between You and Your Husband

*"For you created my inmost being; you knit me together in my
mother's womb. I praise you because I am fearfully and wonderfully made;
your works are wonderful, I know that full well."*
Psalm 139:13,14

Think about It . . .

Because men and women are so different, who's more likely to:

Men	Women	
❑	❑	Call friends and ask if they want to go shopping?
❑	❑	Wear the same pair of jeans three days in a row?
❑	❑	Ask if his or her hair looks messed up?
❑	❑	Turn lawn care into a competition with the neighbors?
❑	❑	Go to a public restroom with a group?
❑	❑	Refuse to ask for directions when lost?

What is the greatest difference you've observed between men and women?

_____

_____

_____

_____

What I've Discovered about Being Two of a Kind

When I first met Mike, I was blown away by all our similarities: we were both firstborn children, raised in Kansas City; he had one sister and I had one brother; we grew up attending church every time the doors were open; we had grandparents who lived in small towns; we loved to go to the movies and the lake; our family values were almost identical; and we both loved God and wanted to serve Him with our life. I remember thinking, *We couldn't be more alike! We are perfect for each other!*

Many dating couples, intoxicated with love, can only see the similarities they share. But once they are married and living together twenty-four hours a day, seven days a week, they begin to see many differences.

We can allow those differences to drive us crazy, or we can learn to appreciate them. After twenty-five years of marriage, I can tell you many ways Mike and I are different from each other. But I still feel that we are perfect for each other—not because we are so alike, but because our differences bring incredible value to our life and family.

Where Do Our Differences Come From?

Relationship expert Gary Smalley shares a fun way to look at the differences in men and women. He describes women as butterflies and men as buffaloes. Butterflies are sensitive, aware of their environment, and perceptive to the slightest changes. Buffaloes, on the other hand, are tough and sturdy—they probably wouldn't even notice a high-speed gust of wind.[1]

Men and women have been different from the beginning—and it is all by divine design. The Bible tells us that God created the heavens, the earth and all that is on it including people. Genesis 2:15 tells us that God took the man and put him in the Garden of Eden to take care of it. Genesis 2:18 further explains: "Then the LORD God said, 'It is not good for the man to be alone. I will make a helper suitable for him.'"

And so God created the woman, Eve, and brought her to the man, Adam—two distinct creations, designed to become one flesh (Genesis 2:24). They were perfect for each other, but even in perfection they were different. Adam was created from the ground and was assigned tasks. Eve was created from Adam's side. She was designed specifically for relationship—created to meet Adam's relational need and equipped to bear and nurture children. God created men and women to bring unique and valuable qualities to each other.

Does realizing that God created men and women differently change your perspective? If so, how?

How Are Men and Women Different?

Every person is created uniquely by God. Here are several characteristics that show how men and women are different. Keep in mind that they are general in nature and may not apply to all men and all women.

Physically

Men and women are physically different in many ways beyond their reproductive organs. Differences occur in life span, skeletal structure, organ size, breathing capacity, physical strength, hormones, and metabolism. Basically, men and women differ in almost every cell of their bodies.[2]

Mentally

Men and women are equally intelligent, but their brain structures are different. Generally, a man has fewer connectors between the left and right halves of his brain. His singularly focused brain gives him greater ability to ignore distractions, while women have a greater ability to think of many things at once. Women are typically better at multitasking, are more alert to surroundings and body language, and have a greater capacity to integrate visual and verbal information.[3]

Because the emotional and verbal parts of a woman's brain are more integrated, each life issue tends to be intertwined with all other life issues. In *Men Are Like Waffles—Women Are Like Spaghetti*, Bill and Pam Farrel explain how men process life issues by moving from box to box, while women process life like a plate of tangled spaghetti.[4]

DIFFERENCE—A man can be singularly focused, thinking of only one topic at a time. A woman usually is able to multitask.

If you ask your husband a question while he is watching television, and he doesn't answer you, how should you respond?

_____

_____

_____

_____

_____

_____

_____

_____

_____

_____

I've discovered these things work in my marriage:

- Politely call him by name, and ask for his attention for a moment.
- Don't try to engage in conversation if he is intensely focused on something else.
- Watch for patterns to learn when the best times are to approach him. For Mike and me, it's when we've set aside time to be together.

Relationally

Because the female brain is more integrated, we may actually attach our identity to our relationships and surroundings more than men do.[5] This distinction is most notable

> Women are more relational by nature.

at puberty, when a female's body begins mass production of oxytocin *(AWK-si-TOE-suhn)*. This hormone supports lactation and promotes a strong desire to build and nurture relationships.

Puberty in males has a very different effect. Rather than increasing their bonds with others, boys develop through patterns of separation and power. While males still find relationships important, they seek to distinguish themselves individually.

As men and women pass midlife, male and female hormones level out. Men generally become more relational and sensitive, while women may become more assertive and independent.[6]

Verbally

According to author and counselor Norman Wright, men and women communicate based on different goals. Men have learned to speak *report-talk*, communicating primarily to exchange knowledge and express skills. Women, on the other hand, speak *rapport-talk*, communicating to create and strengthen bonds in relationships.

Likewise, the language used by each gender is different. Men speak the language of *resolvers*—giving condensed, bottom-line, factual information. Women speak the language of *expressers*—sharing expanded details and emotions.[7]

DIFFERENCE—A man's brain is wired for problem solving, and he speaks the language of a "resolver." A woman typically engages in "rapport-talk," and speaks the language of an "expresser."

If you need to talk (engage in "rapport-talk"), but your husband jumps to problem solving, how should you respond?

I've learned to begin a conversation with this simple phrase, "Honey, I really don't need you to resolve anything, I just need you to listen."

Emotionally

Despite common belief, studies show that men and women experience emotion at generally the same rate.[8] However, the pace in which they process and express their emotions is different.

A woman usually talks to process an emotion because the emotional and verbal sides of her brain are more integrated.[9] As she talks, she is able to find a solution to what she is feeling, usually without help. That's why a woman may get frustrated when her husband tries to problem solve instead of just listen.

In contrast, most men are unable to talk about what they feel immediately after experiencing an emotion, nor do they always find talking about it necessary. Instead of talking, it is often more natural for a man to take action to help him process his emotions (e.g., lifting weights, fixing cars, having sex, going for a drive).[10] But even after he has grasped and rationalized his feelings, a man may still be reluctant to express himself verbally unless he feels safe.

Authors Jimmy and Karen Evans observe that many women will openly share their emotions, yet most "men need a protected environment in which to open up emotionally and begin to talk."[11] The Evans believe that women are physically modest and emotionally immodest, while men are physically immodest and emotionally modest.

This explains why a man may feel uncomfortable and vulnerable when asked to share his emotions before he is ready. Also, if we openly share the intimate, emotional details of our marriage with others, our husband may feel violated.

> **DIFFERENCE— A woman generally processes emotion by talking openly. A man often processes emotion by taking action, and he needs a safe environment in order to express how he feels.**

If you ask your husband how he's feeling after a stressful day and he has difficulty telling you, how should you respond?

I've learned to create a safe environment for my husband to share his feelings by:

- Giving him the space and time to process how he feels
- Not communicating in any way that I condemn or judge what he has expressed (eye-rolling, sighing, sarcasm, withdrawing, etc.)
- Using *action* words rather than *feeling* words—asking, "How does that make you want to respond?" rather than "How does that make you feel?"

Intuitively

Several resources logically explain what some people call *women's intuition*. Gary Smalley comments, "It's not something mystical; rather, it is an unconscious perception of minute details that are sometimes tangible, sometimes abstract in nature. Since it is usually an 'unconscious' process, many times a woman isn't able to give specific explanations for the way she feels. She simply perceives or 'feels' something about a situation or person, while a man tends to follow logical analysis of circumstances or people."[12]

> A woman more naturally notices body language, eye movements, and facial expressions that a man might overlook because he is more singularly focused.

Sexually

The hormones that drive a man's desire for sex remain fairly constant, while a woman's sex drive is usually related to her menstrual cycle. A woman may consider the act of sex to be important, but optional. Her desire for intimacy is directly related to her emotional connection with her spouse.

Shaunti Feldhahn shares the following insights about men's outlook on sex:

- Sex for a husband is more than just a physical need.
- A lack of sex is as emotionally devastating to him as a lack of communication would be to a woman.
- Even with frequent sex, he does not feel fulfilled unless he senses his wife genuinely desires to be with him.
- Fulfilling sex makes him feel loved and desired in a world where he often feels isolated.
- Fulfilling sex gives him confidence in every area of his life.[13]

As you can see, men and women are quite different. But the differences don't stop with gender. We are also different because of the family structure in which we were raised, our personality type, and our "love language" (i.e., the way we give and receive love. For more information, read *The Five Love Languages* by Gary Chapman.[14])

The natural tendency is to focus on what you think is lacking in your husband. What is the result of focusing on your husband's differences?

_____

_____

_____

_____

_____

_____

_____

_____

_____

_____

_____

_____

_____

How Can We Grow in Appreciating These Differences?

Before I understood how my husband and I are different, I would often misinterpret him and respond in frustration or hurt. For example, there have been many times when I've wanted to engage in rapport-talk and build our relationship, but all I got from Mike was a brief report. I felt like he was cutting me off or keeping me out, which was not his intention at all.

Understanding the differences in men and women has helped me to respond more appropriately to Mike. Instead of being frustrated by his responses, I've grown to appreciate them. I try not to focus on the ways we are different, but on the balance and perspective we bring to one another. This new focus motivates me to learn more about him, and I have discovered how incredibly fascinating he can be.

> Once you recognize that he is who he is and you become curious, fascinated, and amazed by him, he'll see it in your eyes. And men really respond to a woman's eyes being fascinated, amazed, and honoring of them.
>
> Gary Smalley, *Secrets* DVD

If we want to handle these differences correctly, we need to create a safe environment in our marriage. Our husband needs to feel the freedom to open up and be who he is without criticism and judgment.

Here are some questions I ask myself to help create a safe environment:

- **Am I accepting his differences as part of God's design?** Read Psalm 139:13,14.

  Answer: _____

  _____

- **Am I remembering that I am stronger with him than I am alone?**
  Read Ecclesiastes 4:9–12.

  Answer: _____

  _____

- **Do I acknowledge when our quarrels are caused by my selfish desires (i.e., wanting him to respond the way I want him to)?** Read James 4:1–6.

  Answer: _____

  _____

- **Am I quick to forgive when our differences cause me pain?** Read Colossians 3:13,14.

  Answer: _____

  _____

- **Am I being patient with him?** Read Ephesians 4:2,3.

  Answer: _____

  _____

- **Have I asked God to help me love him and be fascinated by him today?** Read 1 Thessalonians 3:12.

  Answer: _____

  _____

- **Am I truly thankful for him and confident that God is working in his life?** Read Philippians 1:3–6.

  Answer: _____

  _____

What is an example of how your husband brings balance and/or perspective to your life?

_____

_____

_____

_____

_____

_____

_____

_____

_____

_____

_____

_____

_____

_____

_____

The Secret to Embracing His Differences

We can learn a lot from our husband. As we live with someone so different from us, God can help us to see where we need to grow and to change. The result will be Christlike selflessness and real maturity.

When our husband sees that we embrace who he is (and that we aren't trying to change him), he will feel safe with us. This safety will create an environment for our relationship to grow and strengthen.

God designed the differences between my husband and me to bring incredible balance to our lives!

Verses to Remember

"I thank my God every time I remember you. In all my prayers for all of you, I always pray with joy . . . being confident of this, that he who began a good work in you will carry it on to completion until the day of Christ Jesus" (Philippians 1:3,4,6).

Prayer

Heavenly Father, thank You so much for my husband. May my love for him grow every day. Help me to appreciate our differences without criticism. Allow Your grace to flow through our lives when we don't understand one another. Provide healing for the moments of hurt; help us to be patient with one another and to understand each other more. Help us to complete each other in all the ways You intend. And may we grow more in Your image as we grow closer to each other. Amen.

Notes from the *Secrets* DVD …

Meet Gary Smalley …

He tried to change his wife, Norma, for thirty-eight years without results. On a journey toward appreciating his wife, Gary learned how to create a safe environment in their marriage where they can both experience personal growth. Hear the surprising outcome of his story on the *Secrets* DVD.

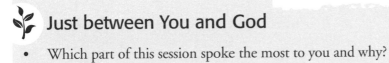

Just between You and God

- Which part of this session spoke the most to you and why?

  _____

  _____

  _____

- Make a list of your husband's strengths, and ask God to show you how your husband enhances your life.

  _____

  _____

  _____

  _____

  _____

- Turn back to the section, "How Can We Grow in Appreciating These Differences?" Honestly ask yourself the questions in this section. Write your answers in the spaces provided.

- Take time this week to pray using Appendix B, "Prayer Guides," and journal specific prayers and Scriptures for your husband and yourself.

  _____

  _____

  _____

  _____

- Ask God for creative, specific ways to express appreciation to your husband this week. To get your creative energies flowing, use the ideas listed in Appendix C, "Creative Ways to Express Love, Appreciation, and Respect to Your Husband."

 ## Just between You and Your Husband

- Together read the section, "How Are We Different?" Underline the differences that apply to you and your husband.

- Suggested Discussion Starter: Together discuss how you have responded to these differences in the past and better ways to respond in the future.

- How can appreciating these differences change your life and your marriage?

Session 3

The SECRET to Genuine Love

Loving Your Husband with Jesus' Love

"A new command I give you: Love one another.
As I have loved you, so you must love one another."
John 13:34

Think about It . . .

Think back to when you were in elementary school and first started liking boys. Did you pass notes to each other? Did you have a friend tell a boy you liked him? Or did you offer to share your peanut butter and jelly sandwich with him? How did your approach change when you started dating?

When you were sixteen, what was your definition of love?

Do you like me?
Yes   No
(Circle One)

What I've Discovered about Romance

As a young woman, I enjoyed the romance of being pursued by a man who wanted to spend time with me. I remember how Mike and I would talk on the phone for hours, and we would make time to see each other.

Romantic love often begins with mutual affection and physical attraction. When a man is attracted to us, we feel valuable and desirable because he has singled us out. Physical attraction and romance are normal, healthy parts of love. But is that all love is? How should love grow and mature with time? Let's explore a greater depth of love that can change our life and marriage.

What Is Love All About?

In his book, *For Better or for Best*, Gary Smalley describes three types of love: affection, passion, and genuine love.[1]

Affection refers to the "in love" feelings of a new relationship, based on another person living up to our expectations and making us feel good about ourself ("He likes me," "He wants to spend time with me," "He thinks I'm pretty," etc.). We can easily "fall out" of this type of love when the other person fails us in some way ("He stood me up," "He didn't call," etc.).

Passion is built on someone's ability to meet our needs for romance and sex. Passion is similar to affection because it's based on someone else meeting our needs. It is driven by our desire, rather than our commitment, so it can be irrational and short-lived.

Genuine love is completely different from the first two types of love. Rather than centering on someone meeting our needs, genuine love focuses on meeting the needs of others. Hear how Jesus described this kind of love:

> A new command I give you: Love one another. *As I have loved you*, so you must love one another. . . . Greater love has no one than this, that he *lay down his life* for his friends (John 13:34 and 15:13, emphasis added).

Jesus' love for us is completely self-sacrificing, and He has called us to love in the same way. Genuine love is concerned for the welfare of another and isn't centered on receiving, but on giving.

Let's imagine it this way: picture your marriage as a house. *Genuine love* is the foundation, walls, roof, heating and cooling systems, and plumbing. This structure is able to stand firm during storms to provide protection, warmth, and clean water.

> Romance, affection, and passion are all components of a healthy marriage, but they are not the foundation for a lasting relationship.

The *affection* and *passion* are the decorations: the paint on the walls, the throw pillows on the bed, and the flower boxes under the windows. While they are important and make your house uniquely yours, decorations change with time and are not nearly as valuable as the roof when night comes and rain falls.

We can easily concentrate on the "decorations" since our modern culture floods us with its philosophies of love in novels, magazines, soap operas, movies, and music. Most of these ideas create an obsession with romance, affection, and passion. But if we take a close look at our culture, we see the results of this focus: impurity, infidelity, and broken homes—almost everything but *genuine love*.

If we stay focused on affection and passion, we will grow more and more self-centered. This self-focused mindset creates an environment for another kind of love, superficial love, which says, "I'll love you as long as you live up to my expectations and meet my needs." Superficial love is a conditional, self-focused attempt at a relationship and cannot produce a healthy marriage.

- *Superficial love* is focused on receiving; it is concerned about our spouse's ability to live up to our expectations and meet our needs.

- *Genuine love* is focused on giving; it is sincerely concerned for the welfare of our spouse.

What Causes Superficial Love?

I have to admit that I haven't always loved well. Early in my marriage, I allowed self-centered attitudes to dictate my responses to Mike—only meeting his needs when I felt he was meeting mine. From time to time, I would respond with conditional kindness or manipulate with the silent treatment. If I had allowed those behaviors to continue, I would have destroyed any hope of a healthy marriage.

We've all learned self-centered attitudes from our culture. In 2 Timothy 3:1–4, the apostle Paul warned:

> But mark this: There will be terrible times in the last days. *People will be lovers of themselves,* lovers of money, boastful, proud, abusive, disobedient to their parents, ungrateful, unholy, *without love,* unforgiving, slanderous, without self-control, brutal, not lovers of the good, treacherous, rash, conceited, lovers of pleasure rather than lovers of God." (emphasis added)

Can Christian women be caught in this self-centered trap of loving superficially? Yes! Here are some possible causes.

Lack of Understanding

The Bible instructs older women to teach younger women to love their husband (Titus 2:3–5). But many women have never been taught. They simply don't understand what genuine love is.

Fear

Many women fear that if they love unconditionally and focus on meeting their spouse's needs, he won't reciprocate. The pain of possible rejection may hold back a woman from giving unconditional love.

Past Hurts

Many women have been wounded, and they haven't yet experienced God's restorative love and healing. Their struggle to cope with their pain hinders their ability to love sacrificially.

Selfishness

Jesus taught, "Because of the increase of wickedness, the love of most will grow cold" (Matthew 24:12). The *Life Application Study Bible* explains that love growing cold is a destructive disease: "Sin cools your love for God and others by turning your focus on yourself. *You cannot truly love if you think only of yourself*"[2] (emphasis added).

How does society encourage a self-seeking life?

_____

_____

_____

_____

_____

How Does Superficial Love Affect Us Spiritually?

Because our culture is so self-seeking, we may not even recognize self-centeredness as sin. The apostle Paul warned us not to ignore the command to love and serve one another, or we indulge the sinful nature and will be destroyed: "The entire law is summed up in a single command: 'Love your neighbor as yourself.' If you keep on biting and devouring each other, watch out or you will be destroyed by each other" (Galatians 5:14,15).

Later in that chapter, Paul defined the self-centered behaviors that come from our sinful nature:

> The acts of the sinful nature are obvious: sexual immorality, impurity and debauchery; idolatry and witchcraft; hatred, discord, jealousy, fits of rage, selfish ambition, dissensions, factions and envy; drunkenness, orgies, and the like. I warn you, as I did before, that those who live like this will not inherit the kingdom of God (Galatians 5:19–21).

Take a close look at the list in Galatians 5. Some of these acts are more subtle than others—jealousy, selfish ambition, and envy. But these acts stem from self-absorbed attitudes and can lead to more visible sins like sexual immorality, impurity, and hatred. These selfish behaviors destroy many marriages every day.

What are some subtle ways to be self-focused?

If left unchecked, how can selfishness grow to destroy marriages?

What Does Genuine Love Look Like?

For a moment, let's put aside everything we've ever learned about love from past experiences, movies, novels, and music. Now let's imagine the Bible's description of what genuine love looks like:

> This is how we know what love is: Jesus Christ laid down his life for us. And we ought to lay down our lives for our brothers. If anyone has material possessions and sees his brother in need but has no pity on him, how can the love of God be in him? Dear children, let us not love with words or tongue but with actions and in truth (1 John 3:16–18).

Genuine love is more than a strong emotion—those who have genuine love actively give themselves for others. First Corinthians 13 gives us a wonderful description of this self-sacrificing love in action:

> Love is patient, love is kind. It does not envy, it does not boast, it is not proud. It is not rude, it is not self-seeking, it is not easily angered, it keeps no record of wrongs. Love does not delight in evil but rejoices with the truth. It always protects, always trusts, always hopes, always perseveres. Love never fails (1 Corinthians 13:4–8).

How does genuine love play out in our marriage? Whether we intend to or not, we may respond conditionally to our husband: "You are supposed to love me, and I will love you according to how much I feel you love me." But, remember that genuine love offers no conditions—it simply loves. It is conveyed in every word we speak, every expression on our face, and even in the tone of our voice.

What are some practical ways you can display genuine love to your husband?

_____

_____

_____

_____

How Can We Grow in Our Ability to Show Genuine Love?

We may be tempted to think, *When my husband starts showing genuine love, then I will too.* But this thought actually reveals that we are showing superficial love. The truth is, the choice to love is not based on the goodness of the recipient, but on the character of the giver. We can be women of incredible character!

Consider the previous paragraph. How is Jesus an example of this truth?

_____

_____

_____

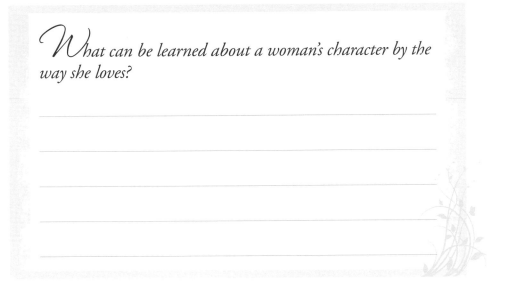

What can be learned about a woman's character by the way she loves?

Growing in genuine love is a lifelong journey. Here are five steps that I continually need to take in order to express Christlike love to my husband:

Step 1 ➤ **Realize that my relationship with God is a journey of becoming more like Him.**

We must understand that being selfish is a natural human tendency, but it is also the opposite of genuine love. We can ask God to show us when we are being self-focused and to help us be more like Him.

Step 2 ➤ **Understand and accept God's amazing love.**

When God's unfailing love floods our heart, He heals our hurts and drives away our fears. Then His unconditional love can flow through our life to our husband (see John 15:9–12).

Step 3 ➤ **Allow the Holy Spirit to lead, guide, and fill my life.**

Genuine love isn't something we can generate on our own. We are dependent upon the Holy Spirit to empower us to love unconditionally (see Galatians 5:22). We will discuss how to pursue life in the Holy Spirit in session 5.

Step 4 ➤ **Make a daily choice to love sacrificially.**

We can wake up every morning and choose to focus on our husband and look for ways to show him love. Remember that genuine love costs us something—the apostle Paul even compared it to a debt (see Romans 13:8). When we choose to do what's right, we can be sure that God will give us the strength to show love even in difficult situations.

Step 5 ➤ **Become aware of what I am communicating to my husband.**

The words we speak are only a part of our communication: our facial expression, tone of voice, and body language can speak louder than words.

We may need to make the following adjustments:

- **Check my words**—are they encouraging and kind, or rude and angry?
- **Check my facial expression**—does it reveal love and joy, or frustration and disdain?
- **Check the tone of my voice**—is it peaceful and hopeful, or critical and grumbling?
- **Check my body language**—is it open and engaging, or rigid and impatient?

What other steps would help you grow in your ability to show genuine love?

_____

_____

_____

_____

_____

What Are the Benefits of Genuine Love?

Jesus challenges us to love God and love others. This is the defining characteristic of all true followers of Jesus. The abundant life He offers can only be experienced as we pursue this life of love.

Joy and Fulfillment

Jesus promises that as we remain in His love, He will fill our lives with His joy (John 15:10,11). We can rob ourself of this joy by choosing to live selfishly. Always expecting our husband to live up to our expectations leaves us (and him) frustrated and unfulfilled. However, we can find no greater joy than allowing Jesus' love to flow unconditionally through our life to our husband! We are never more Christlike than when we love others sacrificially.

Changed Lives

The most effective way to influence another person is genuine, Christlike love. When we are tempted to change our husband by grumbling, complaining, or insisting that he change, we will only push him away. Remember the encouraging words of 1 Corinthians 13:4,8: "Love is patient, love is kind. . . . Love never fails."

What other benefits can you experience by receiving and expressing genuine love?

_____

_____

_____

_____

_____

The Secret to Genuine Love

We cannot truly love our husband if we are not fully immersed in God's love for us. Gary Smalley says, "The number one greatest hindrance to expressing genuine love is when we use our own efforts to try to be loving." (*Secrets* DVD)

> Understanding and accepting Jesus' selfless love is the foundation for expressing genuine love.

God is love—He alone is the source of genuine love! This love is concerned about others and is focused on giving, not receiving. It's a process that happens over time as we learn to lay aside ourself for someone else.

When we express genuine love to our husband, we may not see the effects right away. But don't grow weary—remember love never fails! We can never go wrong by loving well!

Verses to Remember

"Love is patient, love is kind. It does not envy, it does not boast, it is not proud. It is not rude, it is not self-seeking, it is not easily angered, it keeps no record of wrongs. Love does not delight in evil but rejoices with the truth. It always protects, always trusts, always hopes, always perseveres. Love never fails" (1 Corinthians 13:4–8).

Prayer

Heavenly Father, thank You so much for Your unfailing love! Help me to accept Your love. Show me the ways I am self-focused and unloving. I am not capable of genuine love apart from You. May Your perfect, unconditional love flow through my life to my husband. Show me new and creative ways to express love to him. May he feel Your unfailing love through me. Amen.

Notes from the *Secrets* DVD …

Meet Tammy …

She was consumed by her own ambitions to the point of neglecting her marriage. But unexpected news put her on a journey toward discovering genuine love. Hear how God transformed her life and marriage on the *Secrets* DVD.

Just How Self-Centered Am I?

It is difficult to discern our own self-centered behaviors. Honestly evaluate your heart in light of the statements below. Ask God to search your heart and point out any self-centered ways.

I might be caught in self-centeredness if . . .

Circle one

1. I focus on what my husband doesn't do right and the expectations he doesn't meet.

   rarely / sometimes / often

2. I try to change my husband instead of trusting God to work in his heart.

   rarely / sometimes / often

3. I spend more time complaining about my husband than trying to improve myself.

   rarely / sometimes / often

4. I think, *If only my husband would change, then I could be happier.*

   rarely / sometimes / often

5. I move forward with my own goals and agenda, even if my husband doesn't agree.

   rarely / sometimes / often

6. I put my needs and desires above the needs of my husband.

   rarely / sometimes / often

7. I have thoughts such as, *He really doesn't deserve me or all of the things I do for him.*

   rarely / sometimes / often

8. I compare my life and marriage to others and become jealous of what others have.

   rarely / sometimes / often

9. I fail to appreciate my husband for who he is and for the different perspective he brings to my life.

   rarely / sometimes / often

10. I struggle to be grateful, and I constantly think, *I deserve better.*

    rarely / sometimes / often

11. I struggle with ongoing discontentment, and am unable to find peace.

    rarely / sometimes / often

Adapted from a testimony by Tammy Ensey. Used by permission.

How frequently you circled *sometimes* and *often* points to your level of self-centeredness. When we are caught in a self-centered cycle, we are not able to love others with Jesus' self-sacrificing love. We must:

- **Acknowledge that we are self-centered.**
- **Ask God to forgive us.**
- **Draw close to God and ask Him to fill us with genuine, Christlike love.**

Genuine love changes lives and marriages. By allowing God's love to flow through your life, you will completely revolutionize your relationship with your husband!

 ## Just between You and God

- Which part of this session spoke the most to you and why?

_____

_____

_____

- Do you need to grow in expressing genuine love? Turn back to the section, "How Can We Grow in Our Ability to Show Genuine Love?" Which of the five steps do you need to take, and how will you live it out?

_____

_____

_____

- According to 1 John 4:20, your love for your husband is a direct reflection of your love for God. Read 1 John 4:7–21 and insert "husband" in place of "brother" or "one another." Ask God to speak to your heart specifically and to help you grow in your love for Him and for your husband.

- Take time this week to pray using Appendix B, "Prayer Guides," and journal specific prayers and Scriptures for your husband and yourself.

_____

_____

_____

_____

_____

- Ask God for creative, specific ways to express genuine love to your husband this week. To get your creative energies flowing, use the ideas listed in Appendix C, "Creative Ways to Express Love, Appreciation, and Respect to Your Husband." List ways you will try.

_____

_____

_____

_____

_____

Just Between You and Your Husband

- Renew your commitment to love your husband with genuine, Christlike love. Read to your husband 1 Corinthians 13, and say "I will strive to be" in place of the words "love is" and "it" (i.e., "I will strive to be patient, I will strive to be kind, I will strive not to envy").

My Thoughts

The SECRET to
Meeting His Greatest Need

Communicating Respect to Your Husband

"The wife must respect her husband."
Ephesians 5:33

Think about It . . .

You are enjoying an evening out, and you see two couples sitting nearby. One woman leans toward her husband and listens intently. She responds thoughtfully when he asks a question, laughs at his humor, and lights up when he compliments her. The other couple sits rather solemnly. She seems bored and inattentive, actually rolling her eyes at his humor. Then she shakes her head in apparent contempt at one of his comments.

Which husband probably feels respected and admired?

_____

Which husband probably has the most loving feelings toward his wife?

_____

What I've Discovered about a Man's Greatest Need

Did you know that your husband's greatest need is to be respected? Ephesians 5:33 says, "Each one of you also must love his wife as he loves himself, *and the wife must respect her husband*" (emphasis added). I've learned a key marriage principle from this verse: my ability to show respect to my husband will contribute in a significant way to his happiness and well-being. He has difficulty feeling loved without my respect.

> One of a man's deepest needs is admiration. When my wife, Norma, is admiring me, I'll do anything for her.
>
> Gary Smalley, *Secrets* DVD

Gary Smalley explains just how deeply the need for respect influences men: "He hungers for sincere *admiration* and *respect*; he will gravitate toward those who admire him" (emphasis added).[1] The admiration and respect we showed when we were dating our husband are probably what attracted him to us in the first place.

The dictionary provides these definitions:

respect: to feel or show honor or esteem for; hold in high regard; courteous expressions of regard

honor: to respect greatly; regard highly; esteem; to show great respect or high regard for; treat with deference and courtesy

admiration: the act of admiring; the sense of wonder, delight, and pleased approval inspired by anything fine, skillful, beautiful, etc.

The bored, inattentive woman in the opening illustration may have no idea what she is communicating to her husband. Let's look at what a man perceives when his wife is disrespectful.

How Do Men Perceive Disrespect?

When I first learned that men hunger for respect, I realized there were many times when I was disrespectful to my husband. Wanting to understand what I was really communicating with disrespect, I decided to look up some definitions. Here's what the dictionary states:

disrespect: to show or express disrespect or contempt for

contempt: (a) the act of despising; the state of mind of one who despises; disdain (b) lack of respect or reverence for something; the state of being despised

disdain: a feeling of contempt for someone or something regarded as unworthy or inferior

I was *amazed* to discover what I communicate to Mike when I'm disrespectful! I never want to give him the impression that I think of him as unworthy or inferior.

We must remember that men so closely connect respect to love that they will actually feel despised when we are disrespectful to them. Naturally, they are repelled by people who despise them.

Since respect doesn't have the same impact on women, we need to learn what feels disrespectful to a man. The following chart will help us understand some common actions that men consider disrespectful or respectful. You might want to place a check mark next to your most common responses.

> Respect is so important to a man that he might be tempted to leave a beautiful wife who disrespects him, to be with a less attractive woman who admires him.

Disrespect or Respect

Disrespect	Respect
❏ Contradict our husband or question him in front of others	❏ Discuss our questions in private
❏ Openly criticize him	❏ Openly praise him; don't rub it in when he is wrong
❏ Belittle his work or his abilities	❏ Express gratitude for his work and abilities
❏ Belittle his efforts to show affection or help out	❏ Respond with affection and appreciation
❏ Complain	❏ Display a positive attitude
❏ Constantly remind him of unfinished tasks; take his matters into our hands	❏ Give a gentle reminder, then trust him to do his tasks
❏ Act as his conscience	❏ Pray for the Holy Spirit to work in him
❏ Compare him negatively with others	❏ Express genuine admiration
❏ Respond with rudeness or sarcasm	❏ Show respect with tone, facial expressions, and body language
❏ Withhold information	❏ Act honestly
❏ Ignore his needs and desires	❏ Make his needs and desires my priority

*W*hat are other ways a wife might show disrespect or respect to her husband?

_____

_____

_____

_____

_____

*K*ing Solomon, the wise king of Israel, had a lot to say about quarrelsome wives. Read Proverbs 19:13, 21:9, and 21:19. These are strong statements, and yet they give a glimpse into a man's feelings. What insight do these wise sayings provide about how men feel?

_____

_____

_____

_____

_____

Why Is Showing Respect So Challenging?

As women, we may have misconceptions about respect. Some women have been oppressed and abused by men who demanded respect and misused the idea of submission.

> Some wives feel devalued when they are told to respect and submit to their husband.

The feminist movement brought opportunity and equality to women. But some of its ideas have gone to the extreme—teaching that women are not just equal, but *superior* to men. Often popular sitcoms promote this idea by portraying the husband as incompetent, while applauding the wife for putting him down.

These influences may cause us to equate showing respect with being a "doormat" or even tolerating abuse. Or we may believe that showing respect to a man is optional—only granted to those who earn it. All of these subtle, yet powerful, beliefs may cause us to react negatively to the topic of respect. But if we want to find wholeness, we need to understand the biblical essence of respect and submission.

What is your view of respect and submission?

_____

_____

_____

_____

_____

_____

_____

What Does the Bible Say about Respecting Our Husband?

Let's look at the Bible's view of marriage relations. This view was revolutionary for its time, placing the wife and husband in a "working together" relationship.

> Submit to one another out of reverence for Christ. Wives, submit to your husbands as to the Lord. For the husband is the head of the wife as Christ is the head of the church, his body, of which he is the Savior. Now as the church submits to Christ, so also wives should submit to their husbands in everything. Husbands, love your wives, just as Christ loved the church and gave himself up for her. . . . Each one of you also must love his wife as he loves himself, and the wife must respect her husband (Ephesians 5:21–25,33).

As wives, we are called to lovingly submit to our husband's leadership— a way to show respect. Our husband is called to the difficult task of laying down himself in order to care for us. The apostle Paul told the husband to love his wife as he loves himself. This command gave women and men equal value—contrary to Paul's culture which viewed wives as little more than property.

The *Life Application Study Bible* provides great insights about submission:

> God ordained submission in certain relationships to prevent chaos. It is essential to understand that submission is not surrender, withdrawal, or apathy. It does not mean inferiority, because God created all people in his image and because all have equal value. Submission is mutual commitment and cooperation.

> Thus God calls for submission among *equals*. He did not make the man superior; he made a way for the man and woman to work together. Jesus Christ, although equal with God the Father, submitted to Him to carry out the plan for salvation. Likewise, although equal to man under God, the wife should submit to her husband for the sake of their marriage and family.[2]

Why did God ordain submission in certain relationships?

Does submission mean inferiority?

Jesus submitted to God the Father, though Jesus is equally God. How does this clarify equality in submission?

Out of love for God, we choose to cooperate with our husband and respect his God-given leadership. Being submissive to our husband means to voluntarily cooperate out of love for God and respect for the position in which He has placed the husband. However, the most effective marriages find ways to benefit from each other's giftedness. In doing this, they affirm both husband and wife and encourage healthy trust in one another.

How is a biblical view of respect and submission different from society's views?

Are We Called to Respect Unconditionally?

We expect our husband to love us even on our bad days. Even when he doesn't have loving feelings toward us, he is called to treat us in a loving manner (Ephesians 5:25,33). Likewise, we are called to respect our husband even when we feel his behavior doesn't deserve it. We might not admire his decisions, but we can still respond respectfully. This idea of unconditional respect is hard for us to understand and express, but it is just as important as unconditional love.

When we struggle with respecting our husband, we would like to blame our attitude on his inability to earn our respect. But the command in Ephesians 5 doesn't make any conditions except that we submit "as to the Lord." So unless our husband is asking us to break God's commands, our lack of respect is disobedience to God (see Romans 13:1,2).

We understand from Ephesians 5:21 that the ideal for marriage is mutual submission; however, we are still encouraged to submit even if it is one-sided (see 1 Peter 3:1,2). One-sided submission is a difficult path to walk, and only possible as we depend upon the love and strength of the Holy Spirit. We can trust God to take care of us no matter what the outcome is.*

How is genuine love (love focused on meeting another's needs) a foundation for unconditional respect?

---

* When a situation involves sinful and illegal activities or abuse, a woman should seek help. See Appendix D, "Where to Find Help for Abuse."

*H*ow can you show your husband respect even when you disagree with him?*

How Can We Grow More Respectful?

The previous session taught us that the choice to love is not based on the goodness of the recipient, but on the character of the giver. The same principle applies to respect. The choice to respect is not based on the worthiness of the recipient, but on the character of the giver. We can choose to honor God and be respectful to our husband.

*W*hat is revealed about your character when you choose to respect your husband?

As wives, we need to understand that our husband is more likely to crave respect in the areas where he feels the most responsibility: leading, providing, protecting, and problem solving.

Your husband's perception of his responsibilities will be shaped by his personality, strengths, and upbringing. For example, one of my husband's strengths is managing finances.

Typically, men desire to lead, provide, protect, and problem solve.

It's important for me to recognize and submit to this leadership ability, and to express appreciation for his contribution to our family.

---

* When a situation involves sinful and illegal activities or abuse, a woman should seek help. See Appendix D, "Where to Find Help for Abuse."

Here are some simple steps that helped me grow more respectful.

Step 1 ► Be more submissive to God.

The more submissive we are to God, the more He helps us to be submissive to our husband.

> Trust in the LORD with all your heart and lean not on your own understanding; in all your ways acknowledge him, and he will make your paths straight. Do not be wise in your own eyes; fear the LORD and shun evil (Proverbs 3:5–7).

Step 2 ► Understand that my respect for my husband is a direct reflection of my trust, respect, and submission to God.

The way we treat God is usually a mirror image of how we treat our husband. When we are disrespectful to our husband, we are actually disrespecting God. We must understand that God has placed our husband to be leader of our home. We honor God when we respect that position (even when our husband doesn't act respectably).

> The authorities that exist have been established by God. Consequently, he who rebels against the authority is rebelling against what God has instituted, and those who do so will bring judgment on themselves (Romans 13:1,2).

Step 3 ► Ask God to show me how I am being disrespectful.

A friend once told me, "I didn't realize how disrespectfully I was treating my husband, until I realized that I would never want a girl to treat my son the way I was treating his father."

> Search me, O God, and know my heart; test me and know my anxious thoughts. See if there is any offensive way in me, and lead me in the way everlasting (Psalm 139:23,24).

Step 4 ➤ **Learn what makes my husband feel disrespected.**

Each husband is unique—what seems like disrespect to my husband may not feel disrespectful to yours. We should study our husband and be aware of how he responds.

Step 5 ➤ **Ask God to help me to actively show respect, especially when I don't agree with my husband.**

> What a man thinks is disrespectful may not be what *you* feel. Simply ask your husband, *When I do such-and-such, do you feel disrespected?*
>
> Gary Smalley, *Secrets* DVD

While our thoughts and opinions are valuable, we must learn to express them respectfully. When we ask God to help us, we know He will respond. Even during times of disagreement with our husband, God will teach us to show respect in the words we speak, the tone of our voice, and the expression on our face.

Each question below could be asked respectfully or disrespectfully. Practice saying them aloud respectfully.

- *When are you going to mow the yard?*
- *Why did you do that?*
- *Are you sure we can afford that?*
- *When will you be home?*

The Secret to Meeting His Greatest Need

God knows our husband hungers for sincere admiration and respect, so He instructs us to meet that need. We have the privilege of communicating love to our husband on the deepest level.

My personal goal is to show Mike more respect than anyone else shows him. Even when we disagree, I want to meet his greatest need through acts of kindness, submission, approval, and trust. It's amazing—when I'm respectful to Mike, his attraction for me is renewed and strengthened.

As I strive to respect my husband, I will meet his greatest need, and he will be drawn toward me!

Verses to Remember

"Search me, O God, and know my heart; test me and know my anxious thoughts. See if there is any offensive way in me, and lead me in the way everlasting" (Psalm 139:23,24).

Prayer

Heavenly Father, thank You so much for my husband. Help me to understand just how important it is for him to feel respect and admiration from me. Teach me to view submission according to Your Word, and to lay down my life for my husband in the way You did for me. Gently show me all my disrespectful ways, and show me how to express respect in ways that will bless my husband most. Amen.

Notes from the *Secrets* DVD ...

Meet Katie . . .

She had no idea what she was actually communicating to her husband by a small act of getting her own way. But God showed her a simple and profound truth about respect that changed her heart and marriage. Hear her story on the *Secrets* DVD.

Code of Conduct during Conflict

We all need to establish personal boundaries for times of conflict—things we won't say and ways we won't respond. Once this personal code has been established, we can allow these guidelines, rather than our emotions, to determine our behavior.

The first question to ask ourself before engaging in conflict is, "What goals do I have for this confrontation?" If we simply want to point out our spouse's faults or lash out emotionally, then we don't have a healthy motive for the confrontation. However, if our motive is healing, restoration, or resolution of an issue, then the conflict could help make the relationship better.

Here are some ideas to help us develop a personal "Code of Conduct during Conflict."

- **Never threaten the relationship.**

  We should never use the word *divorce* as a threat or attention grabber. Remember, the goal of conflict should always be restoration and resolution rather than hurt and destruction.

- **Do not "walk out" on an unresolved conflict.**

  At times, we may be tempted to walk out in the middle of a heated argument, leaving our husband wondering where we are and what we are doing. If we need some space to cool down or to think things through, we can calmly let our husband know we need some time and tell him where we will be and when we will return. (It is best to simply go to another room, rather than to leave the property.)

What would you add to a "Code of Conduct during Conflict"? Read the following verses from Proverbs and write some personal boundaries in the right column.

Code of Conduct during Conflict

"Hatred stirs up dissension, but love covers over all wrongs" (Proverbs 10:12).

I will not bring up things that were resolved in the past.

"When words are many, sin is not absent, but he who holds his tongue is wise" (Proverbs 10:19).

"The lips of the righteous nourish many, but fools die for lack of judgment" (Proverbs 10:21).

"When pride comes, then comes disgrace, but with humility comes wisdom" (Proverbs 11:2).

"A kindhearted woman gains respect" (Proverbs 11:16).

"A fool shows his annoyance at once, but a prudent man overlooks an insult" (Proverbs 12:16).

"Reckless words pierce like a sword, but the tongue of the wise brings healing" (Proverbs 12:18).

"He who guards his lips guards his life, but he who speaks rashly will come to ruin" (Proverbs 13:3).

"A gentle answer turns away wrath, but a harsh word stirs up anger" (Proverbs 15:1).

"He who answers before listening— that is his folly and his shame" (Proverbs 18:13).

"Do not say, 'I'll pay you back for this wrong!' Wait for the LORD, and he will deliver you" (Proverbs 20:22).

Just between You and God

- Which part of this session spoke the most to you and why?

  _____

  _____

- Take time to reflect on your relationship with your husband. Ask God to show you any disrespectful attitudes, behaviors, or words. Repent and ask Him to help you to grow more respectful toward your husband.

  _____

  _____

- As you interact with your husband this week, consciously check your words, facial expression, tone of voice, and body language. Ask God to help you show respect in every action. (Turn to the "Code of Conduct during Conflict" to guide you.)

- Take time this week to pray using Appendix B, "Prayer Guides," and journal specific prayers and Scriptures for your husband and yourself.

  _____

  _____

  _____

- Ask God for specific ways to express respect to your husband this week. See the ideas listed in Appendix C, "Creative Ways to Express Love, Appreciation, and Respect to Your Husband." List ways you will try.

  _____

  _____

Just between You and Your Husband

- Men are more likely to feel disrespected in areas they consider their greatest responsibility: *leading, providing, protecting,* and *problem solving.* Ask your husband these questions and note his responses below.

In what ways do you desire to lead?

_____

In what ways do you desire to provide?

_____

In what ways do you desire to be the protector?

_____

In what ways do you desire to problem solve?

_____

- Ask your husband, "What makes you feel disrespected and how can I show respect in each of these areas?" Note his responses here.

_____

_____

_____

_____

_____

The SECRET to a Strong Inner Life

Pursuing Life in the Holy Spirit

"But you, [woman] of God . . . pursue righteousness, godliness, faith, love, endurance and gentleness. Fight the good fight of the faith."
1 Timothy 6:11,12

Think about It . . .

One afternoon at work, I hurriedly left the ladies room without checking my appearance in the full-length mirror next to the door. I walked down the hall to my office, passing several male coworkers on the way. About an hour later, I left my desk to greet a group of out-of-town visitors. A female coworker suddenly stopped me in mid-handshake, leaned close, and began pulling on a part of my dress that was stuck in the waist of my pantyhose! I was mortified—and thankful for a friend who was willing to cover my back (literally)!

Describe a time when you were embarrassed because you forgot to check your appearance.

_____

_____

_____

_____

_____

_____

Describe a time you helped a friend in an embarrassing situation like this.

_____

_____

_____

_____

What I've Discovered about My Inner Life

That humiliating experience taught me the importance of checking my outer appearance. I won't ever leave a ladies room without a quick look at my clothing. Believe me, there can be embarrassing consequences when I don't!

The same is true with my inner life. If I fail to look closely at my thoughts, motives, attitudes, and priorities, I begin to relate with others in unhealthy ways. (And the consequences can be just as regrettable as having my dress stuck in my pantyhose!) There is a direct connection between my inner life and the way I interact with others.

How does a woman's inner life affect her relationships?

_____

_____

_____

_____

What Happens When We Neglect Our Inner Life?

The Book of Proverbs describes two different types of wives. Chapter 31 describes a wife of noble character who enriches her husband's life. Chapter 15 speaks of a quarrelsome wife who makes everyone around her miserable. What is the difference between these two women? Perhaps both women have good intentions—yet one is busy taking personal responsibility, while the other is busy trying to get her way.

Who we are directly affects every relationship we have. The type of wife we are is a clear reflection of the condition of our inner life.

We all have difficulty looking honestly at ourself—we tend to overlook the flaws in our own character, but we can easily see them in others. We tend to blame circumstances for our behavior rather than taking responsibility for our responses. Because of this, we can become a quarrelsome wife without much effort. On the other hand, being a woman of great character requires making right choices and disciplining ourself daily.

Think of it this way: our spiritual life is a lot like trying to walk up the down escalator. If we stand still, or coast, we will simply ride down with the motion. In our spiritual life, we have to work at developing our inner self. If we don't, we will begin satisfying our sinful nature, the part in each of us that is soley focused on our own comfort and ambitions. When we start coasting spiritually, we allow our sinful nature to thrive. We quickly find ourself in a downward cycle:

- reacting in unhealthy ways (being impatient, unkind, judgmental, etc.)
- fighting the wrong battles (thinking it is our responsibility to change our husband)
- relying on our natural ability to love, respect, appreciate, and submit to our husband. No matter how hard we try, our ability will never be enough without God's help!

What can happen if you try to appreciate, love, and respect your husband without God's help?

_____

_____

_____

_____

_____

_____

When we receive God's gift of grace, we also receive the privilege and responsibility to live by the Holy Spirit rather than by our sinful nature. Paul explained it this way:

> So I say, let the Holy Spirit guide your lives. Then you won't be doing what your sinful nature craves. The sinful nature wants to do evil, which is just the opposite of what the Spirit wants. And the Spirit gives us desires that are the opposite of what the sinful nature desires. These two forces are constantly fighting each other, so you are not free to carry out your good intentions" (Galatians 5:16,17, NLT).

We can find encouragement in these two verses—we *can* live in the power of the Holy Spirit! Yet, we also find an eye-opening realization. Our choices are never free from the conflict between our sinful nature and the Holy Spirit.

We must actively pursue the right things in order to strengthen our inner life.

How Do We Begin to Strengthen Our Inner Life?

If we want to live in the Holy Spirit's power and strengthen our inner life, here are some truths we must embrace.

Truth 1 ▷ **Many circumstances are beyond our control.**

Spending emotional energy and time worrying about them only leads to frustration, despair, and bitterness.

Truth 2 ▷ **Changing another person is impossible.**

It's a human tendency to turn our attention to others' faults. But if we focus on things we can't change, we will neglect what we can change—ourself.

Truth 3 ▷ **Expressing critical or judgmental words and thoughts hinders the growth of our character.**

When we are busy verbally or mentally rehearsing the faults of another, we are not taking responsibility for our own faults.

Truth 4 ▷ **We are completely responsible for the woman we are becoming.**

Life can be very difficult. Bad things happen to all of us, and all people experience times of trouble or tragedy. But if we blame people or circumstances for who we are, we will never grow and become the person God created us to be.

Once we embrace these truths, what are the next steps? We must take personal responsibility to strengthen our inner self by actively pursuing life in the Holy Spirit. The apostle Paul encouraged us to pursue the right things:

Pursue *righteousness, godliness, faith, love, endurance* and *gentleness*. Fight the good fight of the faith. (1 Timothy 6:11,12, emphasis added).

We are going to look at practical ways to pursue the six characteristics Paul mentions in 1 Timothy 6:11,12, to strengthen our inner life and to help us grow into women of great character.

We Pursue *Righteousness* by Reading God's Word

Since we understand that our sinful nature wants to do what is contrary to the Holy Spirit, we must pursue God's righteousness. How do we do that? We start by believing that: "All Scripture is God-breathed and is useful for teaching, rebuking, correcting and *training in righteousness,* so that the man [or woman] of God may be thoroughly equipped for every good work" (2 Timothy 3:16,17, emphasis added). We need to be women who know and apply God's Word in our life to pursue His righteousness.

A wonderful example of someone who pursued God is David—described as a man after God's own heart (1 Samuel 13:14). David knew the benefits of knowing and applying God's Word, and described them in Psalm 19:7,8.

> The law of the LORD is perfect, *reviving the soul.*
> The statutes of the LORD are trustworthy, *making wise the simple.*
> The precepts of the LORD are right, *giving joy to the heart.*
> The commands of the LORD are radiant, *giving light to the eyes.*
> (emphasis added)

What benefits do we miss when we neglect God's Word?

_____

_____

_____

I've discovered that if I ask myself these questions before reading God's Word, I receive the most from my time with Him:

- Is my heart clean before God?
- Am I willing to allow the Holy Spirit to challenge me and show me anything within my life that is offensive to Him?
- What is God teaching me about himself in this passage?
- According to this passage, what does God expect from me?
- How can I respond in full obedience and apply His truth to my life?

We Pursue *Godliness* by Submitting to the Holy Spirit

Godly living is only possible as we allow the Holy Spirit to lead and direct our life. Galatians 5:25 encourages us this way: "Since we are living by the Spirit, let us follow the Spirit's leading in every part of our lives" (NLT).

When my older son was around thirteen years old, he began to resist my authority. Many times I responded with the same tone and harsh words he used. One day, the Holy Spirit spoke to my heart, *You don't have to respond to him that way. I'm here to help. My love and insight is so much greater than yours. Just rely on Me.*

As I began relying on the Holy Spirit, my relationship with my son changed in incredible ways. I responded to him with supernatural patience and wisdom, and our disagreements didn't escalate like before. I wish I could say that from then on I've lived completely aware and dependent on the Holy Spirit. But I must choose to follow His leading every moment of my life.

> I am 100% responsible for all my emotions, thoughts, words, and actions. If I'm working on myself, it really means that I am working with God to work on me.
>
> Gary Smalley, *Secrets* DVD

God wants us to live with the continuing sense of His presence. The Holy Spirit is able to direct our thoughts and attitudes. He will help us respond to our husband, children, coworkers, and neighbors with His love and insight.

What can you do to live in awareness of the Holy Spirit in every circumstance?

_____

_____

_____

We Pursue *Faith* by Fighting Temptation

The Bible teaches us that we need faith to stand firm against our enemy, Satan. We grow in faith when we know and believe the Word of God.

> Be self-controlled and alert. Your enemy the devil prowls around like a roaring lion looking for someone to devour. Resist him, standing firm in the faith (1 Peter 5:8,9).

> Consequently, faith comes from hearing the message, and the message is heard through the word of Christ (Romans 10:17).

The first time Satan tempted anyone is found in Genesis 3:1–6. Satan tempted Eve to eat the forbidden fruit. Let's take a look at his strategy:

- Satan turned Eve's focus to something she lacked and didn't fully understand (verse 1).
- Satan questioned what God had said (verse 1).
- Satan questioned God's goodness and wisdom (verse 4).
- Satan turned Eve's focus to herself and appealed to her sinful desires (verse 5).

Satan still works in the same way today. He turns our attention to the things we lack or don't understand, especially on our past hurts, our husband's weaknesses, and what is lacking in our marriage. Satan turns our focus inward by telling us that we deserve better. He questions God's truth, goodness, and wisdom, causing us to doubt and fear.

How can faith help us fight the enemy?

- Faith focuses on the promises of God (Hebrews 11:1).
- Faith believes that God's Word is trustworthy (Psalm 119:137,138).
- Faith trusts God's wisdom, goodness, and timing (Proverbs 3:5,6).
- Faith focuses on pleasing God rather than pleasing our sinful desires, and trusts God to provide and meet every need (Psalm 107:8,9).

Consider this situation: You and your husband are experiencing difficulties in your marriage. You go out to eat with another couple. The other husband treats his wife the way you long to be treated. How might Satan tempt you in this circumstance?

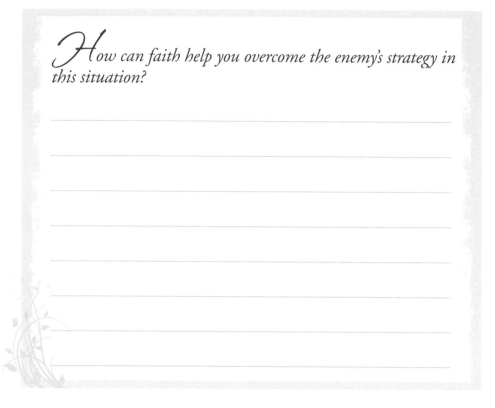

How can faith help you overcome the enemy's strategy in this situation?

We Pursue *Love* by Seeking God

A prayer of Moses is recorded in Psalm 90. He asked God to, "Satisfy us in the morning with your unfailing love, that we may sing for joy and be glad all our days" (Psalm 90:14). Moses was asking God for a daily experience of His unconditional love that satisfies on the deepest level, resulting in a life filled with joy and gladness.

If we want to know the love that overcomes our insecurities and fears and nourishes our marriage, we simply need to know God. God is *love*, and as we seek Him we will actually find love. We can be assured that when we spend time in His presence, His love will fill our life and overflow to others. (See 1 John 4:7–21, especially verses 11 and 12.)

Read Psalm 36:5–10. How can understanding God's unfailing love help you overcome your insecurities and fears?

_____

_____

_____

_____

_____

We Pursue *Endurance* by Embracing Hardship

Most marriage vows include a commitment to endure "for better or worse, in sickness and in health, for richer or poorer." We can be tempted to walk away from this covenant in difficult times. However, as we take the Bible's advice to embrace hardship and not despise it, we will have the maturity to endure in times of extreme difficulty.

> Endure hardship as discipline; God is treating you as sons. . . . we have all had human fathers who disciplined us and we respected them for it. How much more should we submit to the Father of our spirits and live! Our fathers disciplined us for a little while as they thought best; but God disciplines us for our good, that we may share in His holiness. No discipline seems pleasant at the time, but painful. Later on, however, it produces a harvest of righteousness and peace for those who have been trained by it (Hebrews 12:7–11).

When we encounter hardship, we have two choices: embrace it or despise it. Enduring and embracing hardship leads to maturity; despising it leads to bitterness and hardness of heart. Both maturity and bitterness will impact every relationship we have.

How can bitterness affect your life and marriage?

_____

_____

_____

_____

_____

_____

Read Psalm 119:71. What is the value in experiencing hardship?

_____

_____

_____

_____

_____

_____

We Pursue *Gentleness* by Trusting God

Philippians 4 tells us that gentleness is the outgrowth of a heart that fully trusts God. The gentleness described in that chapter is more than a personality trait. It is evident in our attitudes and interactions with others, and is the opposite of being manipulative, controlling, or anxious. This gentleness is the outward expression of a heart full of God's indescribable peace.

> Let your gentleness be evident to all. The Lord is near. Do not be anxious about anything, but in everything, by prayer and petition, with thanksgiving, present your requests to God. And the peace of God, which transcends all understanding, will guard your hearts and your minds in Christ Jesus (Philippians 4:5–7).

The gentle way we interact with others is a direct reflection of our quiet rest and trust in God.

Our inner peace will not depend on our circumstances making sense or on our ability to make things work. It is peace that knows Jesus is in charge, and we don't have to be. When we are confident that God is in control, we do not have to be anxious about anything!

How does a woman who is completely trusting God respond to stressful circumstances?

_____

_____

_____

_____

_____

The Secret to a Strong Inner Life

There is no perfect wife, but the simple choices we make every day shape who we are and determine what kind of wife we are becoming. Remember the escalator example—coasting leads us in a downward cycle. We can let ourself coast spiritually, or we can intentionally pursue life in the Holy Spirit. We can choose:

- *Righteousness* rather than *sinful choices*
- *Godliness* rather than *harmful responses*
- *Faith* rather than *doubt*
- *Love* rather than *insecurity* and *fear*
- *Endurance* rather than *bitterness*
- *Gentleness* rather than *anxiety* and *manipulation*

No matter how far down the escalator we are right now, we can forget what is behind and start pursuing the right things! The Holy Spirit wants to help us (just like the friend who covered my back in my embarrassing story). As we grow more dependent upon the Holy Spirit, our inner life will reflect Jesus' character—and our husband will notice!

Verses to Remember

"But you, [woman] of God, . . . pursue righteousness, godliness, faith, love, endurance and gentleness. Fight the good fight of the faith" (1 Timothy 6:11,12).

Prayer

Heavenly Father, I know that I am not a perfect wife. Help me to strengthen my inner life and to live according to Your Holy Spirit. I do not want to satisfy my sinful desires. Help me to fight the right battles and to focus my energy on pursuing the right things. Fill me with Your Holy Spirit. May I live each day submissively aware of Your presence. Amen.

Notes from the *Secrets* DVD ...

_____

_____

_____

_____

_____

_____

_____

_____

_____

_____

_____

_____

_____

Meet Evangeline ...

She thought she had it all, until her husband made a shocking confession. In desperation, she realized that pursuing God was the only way she could have the inner strength to survive. As she took responsibility for her inner life, she saw God pick up the pieces of her broken life and marriage. Hear her story on the *Secrets* DVD.

Just between You and God

- Which part of this session spoke the most to you and why?

  _____

  _____

  _____

- Do you take responsibility to pursue the right things? Turn back to the section, "How Do We Begin to Strengthen Our Inner Life?" and read the four statements. Then answer the following questions:

  Do you worry about things beyond your control? ❏ _Yes_ ❏ _No_

  Do you focus on things you cannot change? ❏ _Yes_ ❏ _No_

  Do you verbally or mentally rehearse the faults of others? ❏ _Yes_ ❏ _No_

  Do you blame people or circumstances for who you are? ❏ _Yes_ ❏ _No_

- Take time this week to pray using Appendix B, "Prayer Guides," and journal specific prayers and Scriptures for your husband and yourself.

  _____

  _____

  _____

  _____

  _____

  _____

Inner Life Inventory

Pursue Righteousness by Reading God's Word

* How can I adjust my schedule to have more quality time alone with God? How will I protect myself from distractions?

* How often do I read the Bible? Do I actively apply it to my life?

Pursue Godliness by Submitting to the Holy Spirit

* In my interactions with my husband and family, am I led mostly by my feelings or by the Holy Spirit?

* List the fruit of the Spirit found in Galatians 5:22,23. How are these evident in my life?

Pursue Faith by Fighting Temptation

- In what situations am I tempted to doubt? What Scripture verses would help strengthen my faith? (Use a concordance or your Bible's index to find verses relating to your areas of doubt.)

_____

_____

_____

_____

_____

- Is there an area of temptation in my life? How can I stand strong by applying God's truth and goodness to this area?

_____

_____

_____

_____

Pursue Love by Seeking God

- What insecurities or fears do I battle? How do they negatively affect my marriage?

_____

_____

_____

- Read Romans 8:35–39 and 1 John 4:7–21. How can God's love deliver me from my insecurities and fears?

_____

_____

_____

_____

_____

Pursue Endurance by Embracing Hardship
- When I face difficult times, do I allow God to work in me, or do I simply desire the difficulty to end?

_____

_____

_____

_____

- What can I learn from the difficulties in my life right now?

_____

_____

_____

_____

_____

_____

Pursue Gentleness by Trusting God

- In my interactions with people in the last three days, would they say that I was:

  ❏ Kind   or   ❏ Harsh
  ❏ Patient   or   ❏ Impatient
  ❏ Merciful   or   ❏ Demanding
  ❏ Encouraging   or   ❏ Critical
  ❏ Trusting   or   ❏ Fearful
  ❏ Honest   or   ❏ Manipulative
  ❏ Forgiving   or   ❏ Resentful

What does this assessment reveal about the condition of my inner life?

_____

_____

_____

What is my plan to strengthen my inner life this week?

_____

_____

_____

Just between You and Your Husband

- After completing the "Inner Life Inventory," tell your husband your plan for strengthening your inner life. Ask him to help you reach your goal this week.

Session 6.

The SECRET to Growing Intimacy

Guarding Your Heart, Mind, and Marriage

"[Love] always protects, always trusts, always hopes,
always perseveres. Love never fails."
1 Corinthians 13:7,8

Think about It . . .

When you stand in the grocery store checkout line, have you noticed the large number of magazines promising secrets to improve your sex life? How about as you're surfing the channels to find your favorite television program? It seems our culture continually bombards us with images and ideas about sexuality.

Where do many women get information about sexual issues?

_____

_____

_____

_____

_____

What is our culture telling us about sexuality issues (e.g., gay rights, cohabitation, experimentation)?

_____

_____

_____

_____

_____

What I've Discovered about Our Culture's View of Intimacy

Growing up, I was completely unaware that the Bible has so much to say about intimacy and sexuality. Almost every church I attended was silent on this issue. I found that when I failed to understand intimacy and sexuality in light of God's Word, I subconsciously bought into modern views.

When families and churches fail to communicate God's truth, many women look for answers wherever these issues are discussed. I've discovered that many Christian women have bought into secular ideas, and the results can be devastating. Christians experience infidelity, addictions, and broken families nearly as often as people who don't follow Jesus.

Pursuing society's ideas will leave us discouraged, guilt ridden, empty, and broken. But following God's Word will direct us to experience a level of intimacy every woman desires. God will lead us to ever-increasing closeness in our relationship with Him and with our husband.

What Is True Intimacy?

I've learned that true intimacy in marriage is more than sex. *It is the exclusive bond between husband and wife, characterized by affection, warmth, openness, and connectedness.* Intimacy is so much more than physical touch—it is also mental, emotional, and social. This complete intimacy shares hopes and dreams, and the shoulder-to-shoulder responsibilities of life and family. Sexual intimacy is an expression of the warmth, openness, and connectedness a couple shares in all these areas.

> *If we neglect mental, emotional, and social intimacy, what can happen to physical intimacy in our marriage?*

What Is God's Design for Intimacy?

One of God's own traits is His desire for close relationships—to dwell with and be known by us. The whole Bible is God's story of seeking to restore His relationship with humanity. From the following verses, we can learn about the close relationship He desires to have with us.

- Psalm 51:6   He desires complete openness and honesty.
- Psalm 56:8   He keeps track of every tear we cry.
- Psalm 62:8   He desires that we trust Him and that we pour out our heart to Him.
- Psalm 63:7,8   He keeps us close to himself for our protection.
- Psalm 139:1-4   He knows everything we think, say, and do.
- Psalm 139:17,18 He thinks about us constantly.

God had a close relationship with Adam and Eve and walked in the Garden with them (Genesis 3:8). Likewise, Adam and Eve enjoyed true intimacy in their relationship without any shame or fear. Their physical nakedness was a reflection of the complete emotional vulnerability they had with each other (Genesis 2:25). No conditions, secrets, or hang-ups hindered them from fully knowing one another. The Garden of Eden was a paradise, in part, because of the true intimacy they enjoyed.

While closeness with God and intimacy with each other were God's original design, everything changed when Adam and Eve sinned. For the first time, they felt fear, shame, and the desire to hide (Genesis 3:7–10).

> **Because sin entered the world, we struggle with true intimacy.**

And when God confronted them, they blamed and distrusted one another (Genesis 3:11,12). In essence, sin damaged our ability to draw near to God and our husband.

Sin has created a world where we struggle to be truly intimate—we battle fear, shame, and the desire to hide. Thankfully, salvation through Jesus restores our relationship with God. And in marriage, we are able to experience a remnant of the Garden of Eden—to be completely vulnerable and fully known without being ashamed of who we are. This reality is what makes marital intimacy so precious!

Since we are in a fallen world, we must intentionally guard against the things that damage intimacy and drive us to hide. We must protect our closeness with God and learn how to guard intimacy with our husband.

How does God's design for intimacy differ from our culture's view of intimacy?

_____

_____

_____

_____

How Does Closeness with God Affect Intimacy with Our Husband?

I have discovered that my personal relationship with God dramatically affects how I interact with my husband:

- As I enjoy greater closeness with God, it brings the fulfillment my heart longs for and keeps me from placing unrealistic expectations on my husband.
- As I understand God's love, He helps me to overcome any insecurities that hinder me from connecting with my husband.
- As I die to my sinful nature and submit to the Holy Spirit's leading, He enables me to love my husband with Christlike love.
- As I am open and completely honest with God, it prevents me from hiding things from my husband.

*W*hich one of these do you think is most difficult for women to grasp? Why?

_____

_____

_____

What Are Some Ways to Guard Intimacy in Marriage?

Here are five practical ideas to help us guard intimacy based on Paul's teaching in 1 Corinthians 13.

Idea 1 ➤ **Eliminate competition:** "[Love] does not envy, it does not boast, it is not proud. . . . it is not self-seeking" (1 Corinthians 13:4,5).

In his doctoral dissertation on marital intimacy, Jim Vigil writes:

> Ideally, marriage is the only place where one does not need to compete. The husband and wife relationship should be a restful haven. As he protects and provides for her and as she loves and cares for him, peace and a refreshing occur. In sexual intimacy, one does not need to compete but to enjoy rest. . . . Life is full of competition. We constantly have to prove ourselves and compete in the workforce, in the classroom, in recreation, and in life in general. In the midst of this competitive background, we need a place where we can find rest and resign from the pressure of performance. We each need the oasis of one who desires us, knows us, and pursues us for who we are and not how we perform.[1]

Idea 2 ➤ **Maintain personal boundaries in times of conflict.** "[Love] is not easily angered" (1 Corinthians 13:5).

Conflict is a normal part of every marriage. Without conflict, we can't improve, gain greater understanding, or grow. When iron sharpens iron, sparks are bound to fly; times of conflict cause emotions to run high. Without proper personal boundaries, we can unintentionally behave in ways and say things that can damage trust. This harmful behavior will ultimately destroy intimacy.

Establishing personal boundaries for times of conflict—things we won't say and ways we won't respond—is extremely important. Once we establish this personal code, we can allow these guidelines, rather than our emotions, to determine our behavior. These boundaries will protect our husband from hurtful actions and words, and will protect our marriage from damaged intimacy. (Use the guide at the end of session 4 to develop your own "Code of Conduct during Conflict.")

Like trust, intimacy that is actively guarded will grow deeper over time.

Idea 3 ➤ **Forgive.** "[Love] keeps no record of wrongs" (1 Corinthians 13:5).

> For if you forgive men when they sin against you, your heavenly Father will also forgive you. But if you do not forgive men their sins, your Father will not forgive your sins (Matthew 6:14,15).

Forgiveness is not optional; Jesus commanded us to forgive because we can't enjoy warmth, openness, and connectedness when we are reminding one another of past mistakes. Forgiveness must be a continual act in which we ask for God's help each time we feel offended.

We can choose to forgive by accepting Jesus' death as sufficient to pay for our husband's failures. In doing this, we set our husband free for God to work in his life, and we are freed from bitterness and anger. Genuine forgiveness opens the door for renewed closeness.

How does unforgiveness destroy intimacy?

_____

_____

_____

_____

Idea 4 ➤ **Be trustworthy and honest.** "Love does not delight in evil but rejoices with the truth" (1 Corinthians 13:6).

Intimacy thrives and grows in an environment of trust and honesty. When a spouse breaks the trust of his or her partner, the road to healing is long and difficult. For this reason, guarding trust should be a high priority in every marriage.

How is intimacy affected when trust has been broken?

_____

_____

_____

_____

Idea 5 ⋯▶ **Protect your husband's weaknesses in conversations with others.** "[Love] always protects" (1 Corinthians 13:7).

> He who covers over an offense promotes love, but whoever repeats the matter separates close friends (Proverbs 17:9).

One way to establish trust in marriage is to make this promise to one another: "I will never speak negatively about you to anyone." In conversations with others, we can ask ourself, *Would I share this if my husband could hear what I am saying?* Love always protects; it doesn't expose and belittle. When our husband knows we are not exposing his failures to others, an atmosphere of trust can grow.

How Can We Improve Sexual Intimacy in Marriage?

Society's view of sexual intimacy is lust-driven and self-focused—a complete departure from the Bible's message.

God's design for true intimacy is for all of us—whether we already enjoy intimacy or we struggle to overcome distorted views of sexuality. Many women have been victims of abuse or have been exposed to perversion, which can make pure sexual intimacy seem like a distant dream. Others have chosen a promiscuous lifestyle, distorting their understanding of intimacy. But God's redeeming grace reaches to the very depths of who we are and begins to heal every part of us—including damaged intimacy.

> Pleasure seeking needs to be replaced by the one belief that God wants me to love and serve others, because that's where real happiness comes from . . . Life is not pleasure, life is serving.
>
> Gary Smalley, *Secrets* DVD

Since God is the Author and Redeemer of intimacy, you and I should look to His Word for insights that will help us protect and improve sexual intimacy in our marriages.

109

Insight 1 ⋯► **Focus on fulfilling your husband.**

Sexual intimacy is about relationship and selflessness. Real intimacy and fulfillment are found when each partner takes an "it's not about me" attitude and looks to please their spouse. A wife should always look to fulfill her husband and to grow in her closeness with him. Giving herself to her husband and pursuing intimacy with him is a biblical act.

> The husband should fulfill his marital duty to his wife, and likewise the wife to her husband. The wife's body does not belong to her alone but also to her husband. In the same way, the husband's body does not belong to him alone but also to his wife. Do not deprive each other except by mutual consent and for a time, so that you may devote yourselves to prayer (1 Corinthians 7:3–5).

If someone has a selfish perspective, what aspects of real intimacy do they miss?

Insight 2 ···▶ **Keep sexual toys and pornography out of your marriage.**

Many in our culture feel that sexual toys and pornography are the answer to diminishing sexual interest in one's spouse. But according to Jim Vigil, the opposite is true:

> External tools cannot replace a genuine pursuit of knowing the other . . . . Usually those external tools and toys are made to enhance the sexual experience. The danger in this is that the focus becomes the ecstasy brought on by mechanics rather than by genuine intimate relationship. The mechanics can be impersonal and lead to self-centeredness.
>
> Not only is psychological self-centeredness present, but also a neurological distortion occurs. . . . When a person has a sexual release, the brain experiences a release of chemicals called endorphins and encephalins—the highest rush in the human body. Cocaine affects this same area of the brain, which is why cocaine is so addictive.
>
> Because the effect of the chemical release is brought on through a specific behavior, the person will continue the practice. When a person experiences the "high," whatever else he or she is experiencing at the time (whether it is a partner, pornography, prostitution, sex devices, or fetishes) becomes fused with the experience—a bonding occurs.
>
> So if a person has a sexual fantasy, he or she will start bonding to that fantasy world; if pornography, pornography becomes that fulfillment; if through masturbation, the person begins to equate sexual fulfillment with himself or herself—not with his or her spouse. The fantasies, devices, and practices will become the objects of desire—rather than the person bonding to his or her spouse.[2]

> Could it be that God has designed us to be "addicted" to our spouse?

God wants us to associate sexual release with our spouse—bonding us and nurturing true intimacy. Sex devices, books, pornography, and masturbation will never bring true fulfillment. Additionally, because of the physiological responses, sexual addictions can be the most difficult to break. This is why the apostle Paul told us that sexual sins are so damaging:

> **Science is now proving what Scripture has told us for generations. Sexual sin affects the body because of our physiological and psychological design.**

> Run from sexual sin! No other sin so clearly affects the body as this one does. For sexual immorality is a sin against your own body (1 Corinthians 6:18, NLT).

Insight 3 ➤ Avoid fantasy role-playing.

If a wife dresses up or role-plays as another personality, she is opening the door for her husband to fantasize about being with someone else. Why would she want to be responsible for planting thoughts which could potentially lead her husband to adulterous actions?

While a wife should remember to keep her body and attire attractive for her husband, her lingerie should help him focus on *her,* rather than a fantasy person. Likewise, each wife should make love to her *husband*, not someone she's imagined in a fantasy world. Inappropriate sexual role-playing opens doors that are better left closed.

Paul, in the Book of Philippians, gave a principle that applies to this.

> Whatever is true . . . whatever is right, whatever is pure . . . think about such things (Philippians 4:8).

Insight 4 ➤ **Ask God to help you guard your thoughts.**

Because of past experiences and individual design, each of us has personal areas of vulnerability, such as romance novels and various types of music, movies, magazines, or settings. We need to be aware of activities or situations that can tempt us to fantasize about other men, to be dissatisfied with our husband, or to criticize our appearance or our sex life.

We can ask God to reveal these areas of vulnerability and to help us set personal boundaries to protect our thought life. We can pray what King David prayed.

> I will be careful to lead a blameless life. . . . I will walk in my house with blameless heart. I will set before my eyes no vile thing (Psalm 101:2,3).

Insight 5 ➤ **Avoid talking to others about your sex life.**

Sexual intimacy is designed for exclusivity. Only then can a husband and wife experience complete and total trust, complete and total freedom, and complete and total fulfillment.

When we discuss our sex life with our friends, we are tempting our friends to have sexual thoughts—including thoughts about our husband. We also open ourself to unhealthy comparisons. (An exception to this rule is when a couple needs counseling for their intimacy issues—they should talk together with a Christian counselor.)

> But among you there must not be even a hint of sexual immorality, or of any kind of impurity, or of greed, because these are improper for God's holy people. Nor should there be obscenity, foolish talk or coarse joking, which are out of place (Ephesians 5:3,4).

What are other potential dangers of discussing your sex life with friends and family?

_____

_____

_____

_____

_____

_____

Insight 6 ➤ **Ask God to help you desire and enjoy pure sexual intimacy with your husband.**

Just like Adam and Eve, we may try to hide our sexual brokenness. Satan wants to keep us broken and ashamed. But God wants us to invite Him into the intimate places of our life. He has the power to heal, restore, and bless.

Often couples who are newly married can't imagine their desire for sexual intimacy will ever fade. We should always pray that we will desire our husband's touch. If our desire for intimacy has diminished over time, or if past experiences have negatively impacted this area of our marriage, God is more than able to heal and to restore pure sexual desire and fulfillment.

> May you rejoice in the [husband] of your youth. . . . may you ever be captivated by [his] love (Proverbs 5:18,19).

The Secret to Growing Intimacy

As the Author of intimacy, God desires for us to experience life-giving closeness with Him and with our spouse—requiring us to fully trust God's Word and reject our culture's philosophies. Through a gradual process of daily obedience to godly principles, we will begin to reap the blessings of true intimacy.

When I actively pursue God and guard this precious gift, intimacy will continue to grow and become more fulfilling year after year.

Take it from me, a wife of more than twenty-five years: Mike and I have put into practice all the secrets I've just shared, and we are closer today than ever before.

Verses to Remember

"I will be careful to lead a blameless life. . . . I will walk in my house with blameless heart. I will set before my eyes no vile thing" (Psalm 101:2,3).

Prayer

Heavenly Father, thank You so much for the opportunity to know You and to be known by You! Help me to be completely honest with You, and to enjoy the closeness You offer. Thank You for my husband. May our love grow deeper with each passing day. Heal the broken places that may hinder our relationship. Let Your Word—and not society— influence my view of sexual intimacy. Help me do all I can to guard our intimacy so it can grow stronger. Help me to be drawn to my husband, and may I look to fulfill him in every way possible. Today I surrender this part of my life to You. Thank You for caring about what is closest to my heart. Amen.

Notes from the *Secrets* DVD ...

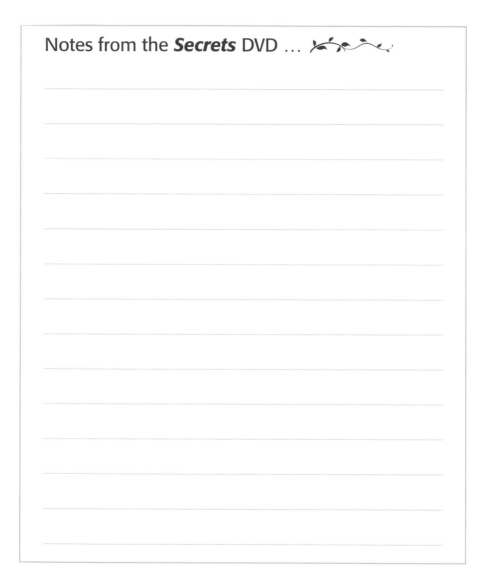

Meet Karen . . .

She searched for a way to resolve the intimacy issues in her marriage and found dangerous answers. A friend's intervention caused Karen to surrender her brokenness to God, who healed her from childhood abuse and restored true intimacy in her marriage. Hear her story on the *Secrets* DVD.

Ten Ways to Create a More Romantic Bedroom

Marriage is the most intimate relationship two people can have. Studies show that genuine sexual intimacy has the power to sustain a marriage as few things can. Rather than being a storeroom for clutter, the bedroom should be a place where love and romance are cultivated, encouraged, and celebrated.

Here are ten ideas to help you turn your bedroom into an incubator for romance.

1. **Put away clutter.** If you want a romantic bedroom, unfinished projects must go somewhere else. Utilize space in closets and under the bed, as well as baskets and boxes with lids. By simply straightening up the room, you'll be less burdened by looming tasks and you'll feel more relaxed.

2. **Don't use your bedroom as storage.** Take time to sort through the stored items and decide which need to be put away, given away, sold, or moved someplace else for storage.

3. **Choose colors that soothe.** Colors have a way of connecting with emotions. If you don't know what colors and styles you like, search home magazines and catalogs. Use these ideas to decorate your own bedroom.

4. **Use many of your best decorations.** Put as much effort into your bedroom as you would a room with higher traffic. Your husband will appreciate the extra attention to enhance your romance.

5. **Use decorations to remind you of special memories.** Items such as dried flowers, photos, framed marriage vows, and special books will continually remind you of how your love has blossomed over the years.

6. **Invest in candles and burn them often.** Nothing gives a romantic ambiance like candlelight. Find several fragrances and colors that you and your husband love, and burn them often.

7. **Spray linens and clothing with refreshing scents.** Linen spray is a quick and easy way to keep sheets smelling fresh, and the soothing fragrances can create a calm atmosphere.

8. **Take out the television.** By removing the television from your bedroom, you open up free time to reconnect with your husband in a special way without distractions.

9. **Play romantic music.** Frequently play your favorite music both to relax and create a loving mood. Choose a variety of music that soothes both you and your spouse, and don't forget to include songs that carry special meanings and memories.

10. **Wear an attitude to match.** A beautiful bedroom only provides half the romance. If you give your spouse the cold shoulder or use the bedroom to manipulate to get what you want, it will not be the warm place of love that it was meant to be. Work to make your time in the bedroom a time of building up your marriage emotionally and spiritually. Pray together regularly, avoid getting into conflicts before bedtime, and make efforts to communicate in loving ways. If you practice these things, no matter how your bedroom looks to the eye, the heart will recognize it as a place of true love.

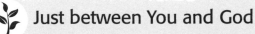

Just between You and God

- Which part of this session spoke the most to you and why?

  _____

  _____

- Look back through the section "What Are Some Ways to Guard Intimacy in Marriage?" Honestly ask God to reveal the areas where you need to more actively guard your heart, mind, and marriage.

  _____

  _____

  _____

- If you have not yet written a "Code of Conduct during Conflict," take time to write one using the guide at the end of session 4. Ask God to help you respond to conflict in positive—not destructive—ways.

- Read the section, "How Can We Improve Sexual Intimacy in Marriage?" Humbly ask God to show you how you can respond to each of these principles. Write your thoughts here.

  _____

  _____

  _____

  _____

  _____

- Whenever you encounter temptation, follow the pattern of Jesus and quote Scripture. Review the verses in this session, and memorize those that apply to your areas of vulnerability so you will be ready when temptation comes. Write a verse you will memorize here.

- Read "Ten Ways to Create a More Romantic Bedroom." Which of these ideas can you implement in the coming weeks? How will you do this?

- Take time this week to pray using Appendix B, "Prayer Guides," and journal specific prayers and Scriptures for your husband and yourself.

Just between You and Your Husband

- Take time to read through this session with your husband. Discuss any adjustments you need to make to enjoy the true intimacy God desires for your marriage.

My Thoughts

Session 7.

The SECRET to Staying in Love

Establishing Healthy Boundaries to Keep First Things First

"So they are no longer two, but one.
Therefore what God has joined together, let man not separate."
Mark 10:8,9

Think about It . . .

Do you remember the first time you thought you were in love? Did you think about him constantly, practice writing your first name with his last name, or invent ways to see him?

If you're married, think about your wedding day. Were you excited, nervous, hopeful, happy, full of anticipation?

What things did you do when you were first in love?

_____

_____

_____

_____

_____

How would you have described "love" on your wedding day?

_____

_____

What I've Discovered about Staying in Love

I love to look at our wedding pictures—they bring a flood of wonderful memories and emotions. I remember thinking, *This is perfect, I couldn't love this man any more than I do today!* Now looking back, I realize that I had no idea how much greater and deeper our love could grow.

I've seen these same emotions in countless brides—my husband has performed twenty wedding ceremonies this year alone! Couples stand at the altar in complete sincerity, pledging to love one another "until death do us part." But sadly, many couples separate just a few years after their heartfelt commitment.

No matter how sincere we are, staying in love is a choice! Love can grow and become more precious with each passing day; but for this to happen, we must pursue the secret to staying in love.

Why does it take more than good intentions to stay in love?

_____

_____

_____

_____

What Are the Right Priorities?

Life can seem overwhelming, and what is most important to us can become blurred. Circumstances can consume our focus, and we can lose sight of the most precious things in life. We must commit to these top three priorities, guarding them with all our heart. These top priorities are our personal relationships with:

1. God
2. Our husband
3. Our children

Our children are precious gifts from God—and you might wonder why our husband comes before them. Children thrive in an environment where their parents openly show love and appreciation for each other. But, children's security is threatened when mom and dad are unhappy and not getting along. If we put our children ahead of our husband, we only hurt our family in the long run.

The best gift we can give to our children is a happy marriage. Our children need to see us making time for our marriage and loving our husband in very practical ways. Not only will we create a secure environment for our children, we will be teaching them the right priorities.

> Some women love their kids more than they love their husband—and he knows that right off, and it strains the marriage.
>
> Gary Smalley, *Secrets* DVD

When a mother puts her children first, what might happen in that home?

_____

_____

_____

If we get any of these top three priorities out of order, our life will not function as God desires. But what about other priorities that need our time? These may change with each season of our life. We should seek God's direction as we establish the following priorities.

- Our career (Our career should always support our family and home, not the other way around.)
- Our extended family
- Our friends
- Our commitments to church ministry and other volunteer roles
- Our hobbies and other entertainment

Even when we make our best efforts to keep our priorities right, circumstances can create a strain or cause them to be blurred (a deadline on the job, illness of an extended family member, a friend in crisis, etc.). According to Gary Smalley, "One of the greatest ways to keep your husband as a priority is to write your priorities and have them visible every day, because the more we think about something, the more it becomes a belief."

In this season of life, what puts a strain on your priorities? What can you do to keep your priorities right?

When the right priorities are established, we need to build the right boundaries with other relationships.

What Are the Boundaries with Our Parents?

Interestingly, one of the first actions of a marriage ceremony is the presenting of the bride. Scripture repeatedly tells us that a husband and wife must leave their parents, unite with one another, and become "one flesh" (Genesis 2:24; Matthew 19:5; Mark 10:7,8; Ephesians 5:31).

Who gives this woman to be united with this man in marriage?

Wedding Ceremony

Before marriage, we are primarily responsible to our parents. After marriage, the relationship with our parents is not severed, but must change significantly.

In *Marriage on the Rock*, Jimmy and Karen Evans write, "When God said that a man should leave his father and mother when he married, God meant that a man was to relinquish the highest position of commitment and devotion previously given to his parents in order to give that position to his wife."[1] The same is true for wives—it is unhealthy to be so attached to our parents that we fail to allow our husband to take center stage.

While parents must take a lesser role, they still play an important part in our life. Embracing our husband's parents can bring joy and challenge. The story of Naomi and Ruth (found in the Book of Ruth) is a beautiful example of a mother-in-law and a daughter-in-law committed to one another. Their love and care in the midst of great sorrow is a picture of a devoted in-law relationship.

While we still show honor to our parents, we must make sure that our greatest time, energy, and efforts are given to our husband.

If our in-laws don't have the commitment of Naomi and Ruth, we should still make every effort to live in peace with them (Hebrews 12:14). All healthy relationships require self-sacrifice and effort on our part. We shouldn't think relationships are broken and beyond repair if they are difficult; we should pray for God's unfailing love to be demonstrated through our life to our in-laws.

We can protect our marriage and improve our relationship with parents by not involving them in our marital conflicts. If we want advice from our parents, both husband and wife should approach them and show both sides of the issue. When a conflict involves parents, the spouse whose parents are involved should initiate conversation to resolve the issue.

What are some practical ways for you to strengthen your relationship with your parents and in-laws?

_____

_____

_____

_____

_____

_____

What Are Healthy Boundaries with Our Adult Children and Their Spouses?

No one prepares us to be a mother-in-law. Horrible mother-in-law jokes are common because so many of us have difficulty with this new role. Here are a few questions I ask myself to keep a healthy relationship with my son and daughter-in-law:

- Do I encourage my child to keep his spouse as the first priority?

- Do I treat my adult child with the same respect I offer to other adults? Am I keeping my personal opinions about his decisions and behavior to myself? (Any effort to control these things will destroy the relationship.)

- Do I avoid taking sides and refuse to allow my child to vent his frustrations about his spouse to me? Do I look for ways to direct my child back to his spouse to resolve issues instead?

- Do I offer advice only when it is requested—and even then, do I remember they are free to accept or reject my input?

- Do I give them the freedom to establish their own family traditions and lifestyle?

- Do I look for creative ways to extend love and acceptance to my child's spouse? Do I communicate that my child's spouse is just as important to me as my own child by including them in family photos, giving equal time and gifts, etc.?

I've found that when I am careful to treat my adult children and their spouses with respect, I am able to build and maintain healthy friendships with them.

What are some other practical ways for you to affirm your relationship with your married children and their spouses?

What Are Healthy Boundaries with Our Friends?

When my husband performs a wedding ceremony, he says, "God has said that 'a man will leave' what is behind him, and 'cleave to his wife.' Then the two can become one flesh. We, your family and friends, choose to accept and support this union as the most essential earthly relationship each of you possesses."

While it is important for us to maintain healthy friendships with other women, we shouldn't put friends ahead of our husband. Here are some practical ways we can increase the health of our friendships.

- Make sure we are not spending time, energy, or resources on a friend that we should be spending on our husband.

- Examine our conversations by asking ourself, *Would I share this if my husband could hear what I'm saying?*

- Choose friends who support our decision to keep God and our husband as our first priorities.

What are the signs that a friend does not support our priorities—God, husband, children? What might happen if we continue in a close relationship with this friend?

_____

_____

_____

_____

_____

_____

What Are Healthy Boundaries with Other Men?

Mike and I have counseled many women who failed to establish healthy boundaries with other men and found themselves in inappropriate relationships. We've discovered that every wife should guard her heart against thinking that boundaries with other men are unnecessary. First Corinthians 10:12 says, "If you think you are standing firm, be careful that you don't fall!"

> Will you love him, comfort him, honor him, and keep him in health and sickness, in prosperity and adversity, and forsaking all others, keeping only unto him, so long as you both shall live? If so, answer, "I do."
>
> Wedding Ceremony

Very few women simply wake up one day and decide to have an affair. Instead, they make little compromises along the way that open the door of their heart to the possibility. We should establish boundaries *before* we find ourself in a compromising situation. Here are a few practical ideas.

Idea 1 ⟶ **Include our husband on some level in all our relationships with other men.**

Other men should know that when they encounter us, they are encountering one-half of a married couple. Wearing wedding rings and displaying pictures are great reminders.

Idea 2 ⟶ **Avoid private encounters with other men.**

Our culture doesn't discourage married women from spending time alone with other men. While this may be socially acceptable, it can put us in compromising situations. If our career requires that we have one-on-one meetings with a man, we can commit to always telling our husband, and staying in open public places.

> If we spend time alone with any man, we gradually open the door for him to find a special place in our heart.

Idea 3 ➤ **Avoid Internet relationships with men.**

These encounters may seem harmless because they are not face-to-face. But emotional attachments can form very quickly with this type of relationship. These emotional connections can be just as deadly to a marriage as a sexual encounter. Generally, affairs for women begin with an emotional connection which leads to physical involvement.

Idea 4 ➤ **Don't be fooled by Satan's lies—affairs are always wrong!**

Affairs don't solve problems, they create more. The issues that lead us into an affair will follow us into the next relationship. We must take responsibility for changing ourself and make every effort to keep away from inappropriate relationships with other men.

Why does changing partners not change who we are or change the problems we bring to a relationship?

_____

_____

_____

What could we say to someone who thinks these boundaries are unnecessary?

_____

_____

_____

What would you add to the listed boundary ideas from the previous pages?

_____

_____

_____

How Can We Know If We're Getting Too Close to Another Man?

Internal Warning Signs: *If I . . .*

- dress with him in mind
- feel heightened excitement when he is around
- compare my husband to him
- desire to spend time alone with him
- secretly hope that he'll notice me
- feel the need to impress or please him
- think of him often throughout the day
- feel "caught" when someone sees us or walks in on our conversation

External Warning Signs: *If either he or I . . .*

- give excessive compliments
- show affection beyond gestures of friendship
- exchange gifts
- spend time alone together
- discuss sexual topics
- talk about our hurts, frustrations, or feelings when spouses are not present
- guard our conversations when spouses are present
- get upset when a spouse seems to interfere with our relationship

What else would you add to the list of warning signs?

Immediately listen to these warning signs! Take aggressive action in the opposite direction by avoiding contact as much as possible. If we are ever unsure whether to avoid a situation, we should choose the more cautious path. If necessary, find someone to keep you accountable. We can never be too careful when protecting our heart and our marriage! (See Proverbs 4:23.)

Shouldn't Staying in Love Be Easier?

Our culture gives the impression that love should be easy and filled with romance. However, the reality is that staying in love is hard work, even if we're married to a wonderful, godly man. The hard work of marriage isn't trying to live with our husband; it is dying to our selfish desires and loving our husband with Jesus' self-sacrificing love.

Once we have entered into the marriage covenant, God's will is for us to remain committed to our husband. We must accept this truth and work at our marriage every day if we want it to be healthy and fulfilling.

We may be tempted to think, *If I just married the right person, love would be easy!* But this is a lie from Satan.

Think about it—what did we do when we were dating? We worked really hard to impress him—we took time getting ready, we planned special moments together, we sacrificed to buy him just the right gifts, we were careful with our words, etc. Quite honestly, we worked really hard to let our husband know how much we loved him.

After we are married, we begin to feel secure in the relationship and we may stop working hard to make our husband a priority. But we need to remember that anything worth enjoying is worth working for.

If you believe society's view that "love is easy," how might you be temped to react when your marriage requires hard work?

135

The Secret to Staying in Love

Our love for our husband will grow and become more precious with each passing day when we:

- make the right priorities and keep them: God, husband, children
- establish and maintain healthy boundaries with family, friends, and other men
- immediately heed internal and external warning signs that we are getting too close to another man
- work hard to let our husband know he is our priority

No matter what we feel for our husband today, if we prioritize our marriage and pursue our husband like we did when we were dating, the "in-love" feelings will return. Let's work hard to let our husband know that he is the most important person in our life.

A Verse to Remember

"May the Lord make your love increase and overflow for each other" (1 Thessalonians 3:12).

Prayer

Heavenly Father, thank You for the gift of marriage. Help me to keep the right priorities and set healthy boundaries to protect my marriage. Gently show me where I've allowed other things or people to be more important than my husband. Then give me the wisdom and strength to change. As I make and keep the right priorities, grow my marriage to be all that You intend it to be. Bless my husband, and may our love for one another grow sweeter and stronger with each passing day. Amen.

Notes from the *Secrets* DVD ...

Meet Becky . . .

She and her husband are Marriage Encounter's national administrators for their church organization. Marriage Encounter is a ministry for enhancing marriages. Becky is dedicated to helping couples make the most of their relationships, and has seen God miraculously rekindle love and restore marriages. Hear her on the *Secrets* DVD.

Relationship Inventory

1. **How is my relationship with God?**

   - Is He my top priority? _____
   - Am I spending quality time alone with God? _____
   - Am I aware of His presence in the busyness of my day? _____

2. **How is my relationship with my husband?**

   - Does he know that he is the most important human relationship in my life? _____
   - Am I spending quality time alone with him? _____
   - Am I putting unrealistic expectations on him? _____
   - With God's guidance, what adjustments should I make?

   _____

   _____

   _____

   _____

3. **How are my relationships with my parents and in-laws?**

   - Do I need to make some adjustments in my priorities? _____
   - How can I grow and maintain healthy relationships with each of my parents, parents-in-law, and sons- or daughters-in-law?

   _____

   _____

   _____

   _____

4. **How are my relationships with my children?**

- Are our interactions healthy and nurturing? _____
- During conflict, am I allowing the Holy Spirit to guide my responses? _____
- Do my children know that I love my husband and that he is my closest friend? _____ Do they see me making my marriage a priority? _____
- With God's guidance, what adjustments should I make?

_____

_____

_____

_____

5. **How are my friendships with other women?**

- Am I taking time to build healthy friendships with other Christian women? _____
- Who is a woman I can learn from? _____
- Am I helping someone else in her journey? _____
- Do I take time to invest in the lives of women who have yet to accept Jesus as Savior? _____
- Do I have a friendship that is working against the right priorities in my life? _____
- With God's guidance, what adjustments should I make?

_____

_____

_____

_____

6. How are my friendships with other men?

- Do other men know that my husband is the most important person to me? _____
- What are my boundaries with other men?

_____

_____

_____

_____

- Are these boundaries firmly in place? Am I committed to them?

_____

- Do I have a relationship in which I need to listen to the warning signs mentioned in this session? _____
- What steps should I take, and who will hold me accountable?

_____

_____

_____

_____

Now that you've finished the inventory, surrender everything to God and ask Him to walk with you as you make the necessary adjustments.

Just between You and God

- Which part of this session spoke the most to you and why?

_____

_____

_____

- Take an honest look at your top five priorities. Are God, your husband, and your children (if applicable) the first three on your list? How do your actions reflect your priorities?

My Priorities	My Actions
1.	
2.	
3.	
4.	
5.	

- Ask God to help you establish and keep the first things first. Consider writing a list of healthy priorities on a note card and keep it in a visible place (mirror, closet door, etc).

- Are you believing the lies, "Love should be easy," or, "Another man would make me happier"? Do you wish you were single again? Ask God to speak the truth clearly to your heart. Love is hard work—and affairs are always wrong! Allow your thoughts and attitudes to be shaped by God, and not by wrong ideas. Use these lines for journaling.

  _____

  _____

  _____

- If you are struggling with your relationship with your husband, ask God for help. How can you pursue your husband like you did when you were dating? Make your husband your top priority after your relationship with God, and just see what happens. Use these lines for journaling.

  _____

  _____

  _____

- Take time this week to pray using Appendix B, "Prayer Guides," and journal specific prayers and Scriptures for your husband and yourself.

  _____

  _____

  _____

Just between You and Your Husband

- Together take an honest look at your priorities. Discuss practical ways to make or keep your marriage as the top priority after your relationship with God.

_____

_____

_____

_____

_____

- As a couple, have you established healthy boundaries in your relationships with others? What are these boundaries, and do your actions reflect them?

_____

_____

_____

_____

_____

My Thoughts

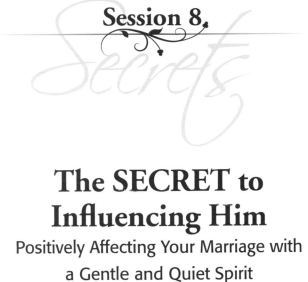

Session 8

The SECRET to Influencing Him

Positively Affecting Your Marriage with a Gentle and Quiet Spirit

"You should clothe yourselves instead with the beauty that comes from within, the unfading beauty of a gentle and quiet spirit, which is so precious to God."
1 Peter 3:4, NLT

Think about It . . .

Someone once said, "If mama ain't happy, ain't nobody happy." While this may be an overstatement, there is great truth in this old adage. In a very significant way, women set the tone in their home and marriage. Imagine the following women:

- Lindsay is a perfectionist who is often critical.
- Amanda is abrasive and often short-tempered.
- Heather appears easygoing, but often manipulates to get her way.

Describe the atmosphere each of these women might create in her home.

How could this atmosphere affect her relationship with her husband and her kids?

What I've Discovered about Influence

As a woman, I'm wired to nurture, instruct, and guide the people I care about. It's a God-given ability so that I can lead my children into adulthood. However, when I allow this mothering instinct to affect my relationship with my husband, he can feel controlled and manipulated. If I try to change him (even with the best intentions), he can react in the opposite direction.

I am intrigued by 1 Peter 3:1–4. These verses describe the powerful influence of a gentle and quiet spirit— the opposite of manipulation or control—and the secret to positively influencing our husband.

To *influence* is the act of producing an effect without apparent exertion of force.

> In the same way, you wives must accept the authority of your husbands. Then, even if some refuse to obey the Good News, *your godly lives will speak to them without any words.* They will be won over *by observing your pure and reverent lives.* Don't be concerned about the outward beauty of fancy hairstyles, expensive jewelry, or beautiful clothes. You should clothe yourselves instead with the beauty that comes from within, the unfading beauty of a *gentle and quiet spirit,* which is so precious to God (1 Peter 3:1–4, NLT, emphasis added).

In this passage, Peter challenged us not to be overly concerned about outward appearance. We should always strive to look our best for our husband, but inward beauty is far more valuable than external beauty. Fads come and go, and our physical body will change over time—but the beauty of a gentle and quiet spirit has eternal value and is always precious to God.

Describe a person who has had a positive influence on you. Was it that person's external *or* internal *qualities that influenced you?*

_____

_____

_____

_____

_____

What Is a Gentle Spirit?

A gentle spirit is an outward expression—it's how we demonstrate Christlike behavior in our interactions with others. Sometimes it's easier to understand a word by looking at its antonyms. Some of the opposites of *gentle* are *severe, rude, domineering, abrasive,* and *unkind.*

> But the fruit of the Spirit is love, joy, peace, patience, kindness, goodness, faithfulness, gentleness and self-control (Galatians 5:22,23).

It's important to realize that having a gentle spirit doesn't depend on having a mild personality. A woman might be mild-mannered and still not possess a gentle spirit—she may be manipulative or anxious. Conversely, a woman who has a very strong or outgoing personality can have a gentle spirit—showing Christlike gentleness when she interacts with others.

A woman who is bold can be gentle at the same time if she allows herself to be led by the Holy Spirit. When she speaks with passion, it is not to get her way, but to benefit others.

All personality types have weaknesses that are revealed when we give in to our natural responses—our sinful nature. Proverbs 15:1 tells us, "A gentle answer turns away wrath, but a harsh word stirs up anger." Natural, careless responses cause us to live with regrets. This is especially true in our interactions with the person closest to us—our husband.

No matter what personality we have, if we rely on our own strength, our weaknesses will be reflected in our actions. But when we die to (refuse to follow) natural responses, we can allow the Holy Spirit to respond through us and influence others with His presence. Only then can we be known for a gentle spirit—and our relationships will be blessed by the benefits of this fruit!

How can an outgoing woman express herself boldly, while showing a gentle spirit at the same time?

What Is a Quiet Spirit?

A quiet spirit reflects our inner trust in God. When we are not trusting God, we may feel pressured to make things happen. We may be tempted to get our way by acting passively manipulative or aggressively controlling.

> In repentance and rest is your salvation, in quietness and trust is your strength (Isaiah 30:15).

Manipulation can be a sign of fear and insecurity. Control often reflects pride which says, "I know what is best, and I need to make it happen." Desiring to manipulate or control others can manifest itself in criticism and judgment. Living like this is exhausting and often produces the opposite of our desired outcome.

Most men react negatively to the feeling of being controlled.

A quiet spirit is marked by inner peace—not a peace that depends on perfect circumstances, but a peace that is confident in God's love and sovereignty. This serenity is present in the midst of life's greatest challenges. We need great faith to quietly trust God, and we demonstrate complete dependence by waiting and resting in Him. Then we find His strength!

How does fear keep us from having a quiet spirit?

How Does a Gentle and Quiet Spirit Attract Our Husband?

Remember that influence is the act of producing an effect without manipulating or controlling. Our life produces a type of fragrance that impacts those closest to us. Whether we are an extrovert or an introvert, people are drawn to someone who is hopeful, encouraging, kind, and peaceful. And conversely, very few enjoy spending time with someone who is manipulative, critical, abrasive, or anxious.

The fragrance of our life affects our marriage in a very significant way. Our husband may be physically attracted to us, but our fragrance will either continue to draw him or push him away. Our inner beauty has much more influence than most of us realize.

A gentle and quiet spirit is *highly* attractive to a man.

Gary Smalley, *Secrets* DVD

Love has great potential to effect lasting change in someone. That is why Peter told women, even those whose husbands do not follow Jesus, that the key to influencing is with a gentle and quiet spirit. Manipulation and harsh words may change people, but only temporarily. Yet even the most difficult person is positively influenced by the encouragement, kindness, and patience of a gentle and quiet spirit.

Why are men drawn to a gentle and quiet spirit? How does this surpass physical attraction?

_____

_____

_____

_____

How Can We Have a Gentle and Quiet Spirit?

Here are some steps I've learned to take to develop a gentle and quiet spirit.

Step 1 ··▸ **Pursue God and allow His character to become our own.**

> In session 5 we discussed the importance of personally pursuing God. The more time we spend with Him in prayer and Bible reading, the more He begins to rub off on us and we begin responding like Jesus.

Step 2 ··▸ **Strive to accept God's love and allow it to flow through us.**

> We can't give what we don't have. When we accept His love, it fills our heart and flows through our life to others. Whether we are naturally shy or bold, God will use our personality strengths to bless those around us. His love will be seen as we interact with our husband with compassion, kindness, humility, gentleness, and patience.

Step 3 ··▸ **Be humble.**

A gentle and quiet spirit is a reflection of a humble heart. Many times our pride keeps us from responding submissively to the leadership of the Holy Spirit and our husband. When we humbly submit to the Holy Spirit, we allow His fruit to be seen in our life. Humility helps us to respond respectfully to our husband with patience and love.

What role does humility play in having a gentle and quiet spirit?

_____

_____

_____

_____

What happens if we simply try to have a gentle and quiet spirit without the help of the Holy Spirit?

_____

_____

Step 4 ▸ **Make our requests known to God and allow His peace to guide our interactions with others.**

We cannot have a gentle and quiet spirit if we are anxious. But as our trust in God grows, we come to understand that we don't have to change people or make things happen. Our peace will not depend upon our circumstances making sense or upon our ability to make things work out. Rather, we can experience a peace that knows, "Jesus is in charge, and I don't have to be."

Let your gentleness be evident to all. The Lord is near. Do not be anxious about anything, but in everything, by prayer and petition, with thanksgiving, present your requests to God. And the peace of God, which transcends all understanding, will guard your hearts and your minds in Christ Jesus (Philippians 4:5–7).

Gentleness is the natural, unforced response of a person who is fully resting in God.

How does worry prevent us from having a gentle and quiet spirit?

_____

_____

Step 5 ➤ **Be quick to listen and slow to speak.**

Epictetus, a Stoic philosopher in ancient Greece, said, "Could it be possible that we are to listen twice as much as we are to speak, since we have two ears and only one mouth?" A wife with a gentle and quiet spirit will listen thoroughly before responding. Only as we allow the peace of God to calm our anxious hearts can we follow this advice:

> Everyone should be quick to listen, slow to speak and slow to become angry (James 1:19).

I've discovered that when I take these steps to actively pursue a gentle and quiet spirit, I am better able to do all that we have covered in the previous sessions:

- Free my husband from unrealistic expectations by completely trusting God to meet my deepest needs

- Appreciate my husband the way he is and trust God to work in his life

- Love my husband as I rest in Jesus' love

- Submit to my husband's leadership and show him the unconditional respect he craves, because I trust God for the outcome in every situation

- Humbly take personal responsibility to grow and strengthen my inner life

- Be drawn to my husband and protect my intimacy with him

- Keep right priorities and maintain healthy boundaries to protect my love for my husband

The Secret to Influencing Our Husband

We must choose each day to do the things that grow a gentle and quiet spirit in us. The choice is ours—we can coast and allow our weaknesses and fears to drive us, or we can allow the Holy Spirit to live in and through us.

Peter encouraged us to be known for a gentle and quiet spirit. Just as we choose what to wear each morning, we must daily choose to follow the Holy Spirit's leading and trust God fully. Not only will we experience incredible personal benefits, but our husband will be drawn to us and be greatly influenced by our pure and reverent life.

> I must daily choose to put on a gentle and quiet spirit.

This truth can be experienced by every woman, no matter what personality. Some of us are outgoing and loud, others are more reserved and soft-spoken. Quite honestly, our personalities are as varied as the unique designs of snow-flakes. God created you to be uniquely you. He doesn't want to change your personality type, but He wants all of us to respond like Jesus and to rest completely in His unfailing love.

Each of us can be known for a gentle and quiet spirit!

Verses to Remember

"Don't be concerned about the outward beauty of fancy hairstyles, expensive jewelry, or beautiful clothes. You should clothe yourselves instead with the beauty that comes from within, the unfading beauty of a gentle and quiet spirit, which is so precious to God" (1 Peter 3:3,4, NLT).

Prayer

Heavenly Father, thank You for the opportunity to know You and to be known by You! Please search my heart and show me any ways that are displeasing to You. I repent for being too focused on external beauty at times or neglecting the inner beauty that is precious to You. Help me to grow more like You as I pursue You every day. May I be known for a gentle and quiet spirit—pleasing both You and my husband. Amen.

Notes from the *Secrets* DVD …

Meet Eleanor . . .

After accepting Christ, she and her mother were nearly kicked out by her alcoholic father. For sixteen years, she watched her mother show him kindness and patiently pray for him to change. Hear about the lasting impact of a wife's powerful and gentle influence on the *Secrets* DVD.

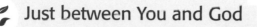

Just between You and God

- Which part of this session spoke the most to you and why?

- Describe the tone that most often characterizes your home (light-hearted, tense, graceful, sterile, emotional, etc). Now think about the tone in your spirit on most days. How does this affect the tone in your home? Ask God to show you if you should change and how.

- If your husband described you in one sentence, what would he say? How would you want him to describe and remember you? Ask God to show you what changes you need to make to become that person. What can you do today, this week, and this month?

- When things are not going as you'd like, how do you typically feel and respond? Do you tend to manipulate or control? How does this reflect your inner trust in God?

  _____

  _____

  _____

- Ask God to show you what areas you need to trust Him more. Finish the following statements to help you identify these areas:

  "I feel out of control when . . ."

  _____

  _____

  "I feel the most anxiety when . . ."

  _____

  _____

  "I feel the most frustrated when . . ."

  _____

  _____

  "It's most difficult for me to show gentleness when . . ."

  _____

  _____

"I feel afraid when . . ."

_____

_____

"I try to manipulate things when . . ."

_____

_____

• Look over the section, "How Can We Have a Gentle and Quiet Spirit?" Which of the five steps do you need to focus on this week?

_____

_____

_____

_____

• How would having a gentle and quiet spirit impact your relationship with your husband?

_____

_____

_____

_____

_____

- Take time this week to pray using Appendix B, "Prayer Guides," and journal specific prayers and Scriptures for your husband and yourself.

_____

_____

_____

_____

_____

_____

_____

_____

Which session was the most eye-opening and challenging to you? How would a gentle and quiet spirit help you to apply the truths of that session?

_____

_____

_____

_____

_____

_____

Which session was the most insightful and encouraging to you, and why?

_____

_____

_____

_____

_____

_____

Just Between You and Your Husband

Ask your husband the following questions for a meaningful discussion.

- "Are there things I do that make you feel controlled or manipulated? If so, how does that make you want to respond?"

- "Who has had a positive influence on you, and what did that person do to influence you?"

- "Has our relationship changed since I began reading *Secrets*? If so, how?"

- Things my husband shared that I want to remember:

_____

_____

_____

Appendix A

Following Jesus

1. **God has a plan for your life.**
   Your life did not happen by chance. Psalm 139:13 says that God was working in your life even before you were born. God loves you. You are special to Him, and He has a special purpose for your life in this world and for your everlasting life in heaven!

2. **God's plan cannot happen for you because of your sin.**
   The Bible says that "All have sinned and fall short of the glory of God" (Romans 3:23). Sin is disobeying God's laws and not doing what He wants you to do.

   We all know in our heart that we have sinned. Even if we have never read a Bible, we can know we are a sinner, because God created each of us with a conscience. We know what we don't want others to do to us—steal, lie, or be unkind. When we do to someone what we don't want done to us, our conscience lets us know we have done wrong. That is why everyone is guilty of sin.

3. **You must be forgiven to have God's plan for your life.**
   When people sin, they must be punished. The Bible says the punishment for sin is death (Romans 6:23). This is more than just your body dying—it means your spirit, which lives forever, will be in everlasting punishment in hell. Jesus explained hell is like a "lake of fire," and that everyone who goes there is separated from God forever and burns in fire that never ends (Mark 9:47,48). Your sin separates you from God both in this life and for eternity.

You can't experience God's plan for your life when you are separated from Him. Many things in your life have gone wrong because of your sin. God still has a plan for you even though you have sinned, but your sin must be forgiven to allow His plan to happen.

4. **God made a way for you to be forgiven.**
John 3:16–18 says, "God loved the world so much that he gave his one and only Son, so that everyone who believes in him will not perish but have eternal life. God sent his Son into the world not to judge the world, but to save the world through him. There is no judgment against anyone who believes in him. But anyone who does not believe in him has already been judged for not believing in God's one and only Son" (NLT).

Two thousand years ago, Jesus Christ, the holy Son of God, became a man. For thirty-three years, He lived without sinning. Men lied about Him, judged Him guilty of things He had never done, and hung Him on a cross to die. Jesus never sinned, but He was punished for sin. Death had no power over Him, and He came back to life after three days! To anyone who accepts Him as the only way to God, Jesus gives forgiveness and everlasting life in heaven.

5. **You can begin a new life today.**
You can receive Jesus as your Savior right now, this moment! You don't have to be in a church or special place, or have the help of a minister or priest. The Bible simply says that "If you confess with your mouth that Jesus is Lord and believe in your heart that God raised him from the dead, you will be saved" (Romans 10:9, NLT).

You can pray now, wherever you are. God is listening. Tell Him in your own words that you are sorry for your sins, and you want to receive Jesus Christ as your Savior (who saves you from your sins) and Lord (who leads your daily choices). Ask God to change your heart and life. It's your prayer He wants to hear. You can pray the following prayer, but it is not enough just to say the words. You must mean it from your heart.

God, I know I have sinned. I believe Your Son, Jesus Christ, died to take the punishment for my sin. I believe Jesus came back to life and has the power to forgive my sin and change my life. Forgive me. Come into my life and change me. I want to live for You and follow Your plan for my life. I believe You have forgiven me, and I thank You for hearing my prayer. In Jesus' name. Amen.

God has forgiven you if you prayed this prayer and meant it from your heart. Now you can begin the life He has planned for you, and you will enjoy everlasting life with Him in heaven! Step-by-step, God will lead you to what He has chosen for you. He will show you the way to live and will teach you each day as you grow spiritually and become the person He planned for you to be.

By Randy Hurst, commissioner of evangelism for the Assemblies of God and director of communications for Assemblies of God World Missions.

From "How to Follow Christ," www.followchrist.ag.org. Copyright ©1997 Randy Hurst. Adapted and used by permission.

Appendix B

Prayer Guides
Scriptures to Pray for Your Husband and Yourself

These are only a few verses to help direct your prayers. As you read God's Word, allow the Holy Spirit to breathe faith into your heart. Allow Him to direct you to Scriptures to pray specifically for your husband and yourself. Record your prayers in a journal.

For Your Husband . . .

Relationship with God

- **Psalm 19:1–4** Pray your husband will see God at work in all creation.
- **Psalm 42** Pray your husband will be "thirsty for God."
- **Psalm 103:1–18** Pray for your husband to experience God's great love.
- **Psalm 139:1–18** Remember that this truth applies to your husband as you pray for him.
- **Isaiah 55** Pray your husband will seek God with his whole heart and find the satisfaction that only God can give.
- **Colossians 1:15–20** Pray your husband will come to know Christ as He is described in these verses.
- **1 Thessalonians 4:13–18** Pray your husband will live in awareness of Christ's return.

Righteous Living

- **Psalm 1** Pray your husband will be a righteous and "blessed man."
- **Psalm 32** Pray your husband will be quick to repent.
- **Proverbs 4:23–27** Pray your husband will be a man of integrity.
- **1 Thessalonians 4:3–8** Pray your husband will avoid sexual immorality.
- **Hebrews 4:12** Pray that your husband's heart will be touched in a life-changing way anytime he hears the Word of God.

Ability as a Husband

- **Ephesians 5:25–33** Pray your husband's love for you will grow to be like Christ's.
- **Philippians 2:1–8** Pray your husband will serve others with a humble heart.

Wisdom for Decisions

- **Psalm 62** Pray your husband will place his hope and trust in God.
- **Psalm 86:1–7** and **Psalm 107** Pray that when your husband is in trouble, he will call out to God.
- **Proverbs 2** Pray your husband will grow in wisdom, insight, and understanding.

If Your Husband Is Not Yet a Christian

- **Hebrews 11:1** Remember that faith is being sure of what we hope for and certain of what we do not see. Have faith in God and believe for your husband's salvation.
- **2 Peter 3:8,9** Remember God's patience and His desire for your husband to come to know Him.

For Yourself . . .

Relationship with God

- **Psalm 33:20–22** Allow God's unfailing love to rest on you so your hope in Him may grow.
- **Psalm 37:1–11** Pray for a greater desire to delight yourself in God.
- **Psalm 63** Ask for a greater desire for God, resulting in finding fulfillment in Him.
- **Psalm 105:1–4** Be thankful and rejoice in Him!
- **Ephesians 3:16 through 4:3** Pray to be secure in God's love and to be able to show His gentleness.

Wisdom and God's Word

- **Psalm 19:7–11** Allow God's Word to revive you, make you wise, and give you joy.
- **Psalm 25** Ask God to guide and teach you.
- **Psalm 119:9–16** Ask God to help you hide His Word in your heart.
- **Ephesians 6:10–18** Remember that many battles are spiritual; allow these verses to instruct and strengthen you to stand firm.

Speech

- **Psalm 141:3,8** Pray that God will help you guard your speech and keep your eyes on Him.
- **Ephesians 4:29–32** Pray that your verbal responses to your husband will be appropriate.
- **James 1:19,20** Pray you will be quick to listen, slow to speak, and slow to become angry.
- **James 4:11,12** Ask God to help you not to speak negatively about your husband.

Ability as a Wife

- **Psalm 139:23,24** Ask God to search you and point out any areas offensive to Him.
- **Galatians 5:22–26** Pray for the fruit of the Spirit to be evident in your life and in your relationship with your husband.
- **Philippians 2:3–18** Pray for an increased capacity to humbly serve your husband.
- **Colossians 3:12–15** Pray for God's help in forgiving your spouse.
- **1 Thessalonians 3:12,13** May the Lord make your love increase and overflow for your husband.
- **1 Peter 3:8–12** Pray for the desire and capacity to seek peace and pursue it.
- **1 Peter 4:7–11** Ask God for a greater capacity to love your husband.

Confidence and Trust

- **Psalm 27:13,14** Pray for greater confidence as you wait on God.
- **Psalm 46** Ask for the faith to be still and know that He is God.
- **Psalm 62:5–8,11,12** Pray for a greater ability to trust in God and find rest in Him.
- **Psalm 130** Be encouraged as you put your hope in God.
- **Philippians 4:4–9** Allow God's peace to guard your heart.
- **Philippians 4:11–13** Ask for contentment.
- **1 Peter 5:7** Allow the knowledge that He cares for you to bring you great peace and comfort.

Appendix C

Creative Ways to Express Love, Appreciation, and Respect to Your Husband

Say it . . .

- Send him a "love" e-mail or text message.

- Talk about how much you appreciate him in front of your family.

- Write a love note and put it in his wallet or sock drawer, or on his mirror, car dashboard, coffee maker, or pillow.

- Send him a card and enclose a picture of the two of you; share with him a special memory from when the picture was taken.

- Ask your school-age children to make a card that starts, "Something I love about my dad . . ."

- Keep a journal of the things you appreciate about him on his dresser. When you add a new entry, leave the journal open so he can read it.

Plan it . . .

- Plan a surprise outing to his favorite sporting event.

- Ask him to lunch and share your appreciation for him during the meal.

- Plan a romantic evening after the kids are in bed—or better yet, get a babysitter so the two of you can spend an entire evening together.

- Plan a nature walk or neighborhood walk for just the two of you, and express how much you appreciate and respect him.

- Invite him for a picnic lunch at a favorite nature spot.

- Plan a day at a lake where you can fish, canoe, or read a book together.

Show it . . .

- Give him a back rub and tell him how much you love him.

- Allow him to watch a game or favorite television show without any interruptions.

- Make his favorite meal and use the time together to encourage him.

- Sing a special love song to him or play it from a CD.

- Decorate and frame a list of his strengths using scrapbook materials and masculine colors.

- Bring him breakfast in bed on his day off.

- Buy him a gift that represents one of his strengths, and write your appreciation for this strength in a card to give with the gift.

My Ideas

Appendix D

Where to Find Help for Abuse

If you are in immediate danger, call 9-1-1.

Abuse happens in every culture, every country, and every age group. But no one deserves to be abused or threatened. If you are being abused, you may feel frightened, hurt, confused, disappointed, angry, ashamed, or hopeless. You cannot stop your partner's abuse, but you can find help and support for yourself and your children. Here are steps you can do:

- Talk with somebody you trust—a friend or relative, someone from your job, a pastor, or a counselor.

- Put together an emergency kit of items you would need if you had to leave suddenly—identification, medicine, keys, money, phone numbers, medical records, children's belongings, etc.

- Call the National Domestic Violence Hotline at 1-800-799-SAFE (7233) to find out about domestic violence shelters and programs in your area (or visit www.ndvh.org).

- Call the National Sexual Assault Hotline at 1-800-656-HOPE (4673) to get help and guidance about sexual assault (or visit www.rainn.org).

- Cut out the cards on the next page. Carry these emergency phone numbers with you at all times (and give copies to your children).

What the Bible Says about Abuse

The Bible does not teach that people may abuse one another. We are God's children and deserve to be treated accordingly. God commands us to love our neighbors as ourselves, and our closest neighbors are our spouse and children. The apostle Paul taught that family members, out of devotion to Christ, can and should demonstrate mutual love and respect.

> The LORD is close to the brokenhearted;
> he rescues those whose spirits are crushed.
> (Psalm 34:18, NLT)

In an emergency, call 9-1-1

National Domestic Violence Hotline
1-800-799-SAFE (7233)
TTY 1-800-787-3224
www.ndvh.org

National Sexual Assault Hotline
1-800-656-HOPE (4673)
www.rainn.org

In an emergency, call 9-1-1

Other Important Phone Numbers:

_____
_____
_____
_____

In an emergency, call 9-1-1

National Domestic Violence Hotline
1-800-799-SAFE (7233)
TTY 1-800-787-3224
www.ndvh.org

National Sexual Assault Hotline
1-800-656-HOPE (4673)
www.rainn.org

In an emergency, call 9-1-1

Other Important Phone Numbers:

_____
_____
_____
_____

In an emergency, call 9-1-1

National Domestic Violence Hotline
1-800-799-SAFE (7233)
TTY 1-800-787-3224
www.ndvh.org

National Sexual Assault Hotline
1-800-656-HOPE (4673)
www.rainn.org

In an emergency, call 9-1-1

Other Important Phone Numbers:

_____
_____
_____
_____

In an emergency, call 9-1-1

National Domestic Violence Hotline
1-800-799-SAFE (7233)
TTY 1-800-787-3224
www.ndvh.org

National Sexual Assault Hotline
1-800-656-HOPE (4673)
www.rainn.org

In an emergency, call 9-1-1

Other Important Phone Numbers:

_____
_____
_____
_____

Notes

Session 1: The Secret to Finding True Fulfillment

1. Jimmy and Karen Evans, *Marriage on the Rock* (Ventura: Gospel Light, 2006), 20.

Session 2: The Secret to Embracing His Differences

1. Gary Smalley, *For Better or for Best: Understanding Your Husband,* rev. ed. (Grand Rapids: Zondervan, 1988), 28, 29.

2. Ibid., 31, 32.

3. Beverly White Hislop, *Shepherding a Woman's Heart: A New Model for Effective Ministry to Women* (Chicago: Moody Publishers, 2007), 59.

4. Bill and Pam Farrel, *Men Are Like Waffles—Women Are Like Spaghetti* (Eugene, OR: Harvest House Publishers, 2007).

5. Smalley, 30.

6. Hislop, 60–7.

7. H. Norman Wright, *Communication: Key to Your Marriage* (Ventura, CA: Regal Books, 2000), 140, 142.

8. Bill and Pam Farrel, *Why Men and Women Act the Way They Do* (Eugene, OR: Harvest House Publishers, 2003), 38.

9. Hislop, 60.

10. Wright, 137, 138.

11. Evans, *Marriage on the Rock*, 216, 217.

12. Smalley, 34.

13. Shaunti Feldhahn, *For Women Only: What You Need to Know About the Inner Lives of Men* (Colorado Springs: Multnomah Publishers, 1996), 92–103.

14. Gary Chapman, *The Five Love Languages: How to Express Heartfelt Commitment to Your Mate* (Chicago: Moody Publishers, 1992).

Session 3: The Secret to Genuine Love

1. Smalley, 69, 70.

2. *Life Application Study Bible,* NIV (Wheaton, IL: Tyndale House, 2005), 1585.

Session 4: The Secret to Meeting His Greatest Need

1. Smalley, 87.

2. *Life Application Study Bible,* NIV, 1930.

Session 6: The Secret to Growing Intimacy

1. Jim P. Vigil, "Naked But Not Ashamed: A Theology of Marital Intimacy" (doctoral thesis, Trinity Evangelical Divinity School, 2007).

2. Ibid.

Session 7: The Secret to Staying in Love

1. Evans, *Marriage on the Rock*, 19, 20.

Permissions

Sessions 1, 2, and 7 include material:

From *Marriage on the Rock* by Jimmy and Karen Evans, pages 19, 20. Copyright © 2006 by Gospel Light (or Regal Books), Ventura, CA 93003. Used by permission.

Session 2 includes material:

From *Shepherding a Woman's Heart: A New Model for Effective Ministry to Women*, page 59. Copyright © 2007 by Beverly White Hislop. Published by Moody Publishers, Chicago, IL. Used by permission.

From *Men Are Like Waffles—Women Are Like Spaghetti*. Copyright © 2007 by Bill and Pam Farrel. Published by Harvest House Publishers, Eugene, OR. Used by permission.

From *Communication: Key to Your Marriage*, page 140, 142. Copyright © 2000 by H. Norman Wright. Published by Regal Books, Ventura, CA. Used by permission. All rights reserved.

From *Why Men and Women Act the Way They Do*, page 38. Copyright © 2003 by Bill and Pam Farrel. Published by Harvest House Publishers, Eugene, OR. Used by permission.

Share *Secrets* with Your Friends!

If you really want to get the most from this study, purchase the *Secrets* **Leader Kit** and invite your friends to join you!

The *Secrets* **DVD** includes eight 20-minute video segments containing:
- Amazing insights from author Kerry Clarensau
- Interviews with relationship expert Gary Smalley
- Inspiring testimonies from wives like you
- **Bonus:** Promotional video clips to play at your church

The *Secrets* **CD-ROM** helps you lead an interactive study in your church and community:
- Options for 8–, 10–, or 12–week small group studies
- Simple notes and outlines for each meeting
- Tips for ministering to wives in various situations
- Reproducible invitations, posters, prayer cards, and more

Order online at **www.SecretsBibleStudy.com**.